CHANGE
MANAGEMENT
The Essentials

The modern playbook for new and
experienced practitioners

LENA ROSS

CHANGE
MANAGEMENT

The Essentials

The modern playbook for new
and experienced practitioners

Disclaimer

The information in this book is designed to provide helpful information on the subjects discussed, and the material does not represent professional advice. The author disclaims any liability to any person arising directly or indirectly from the use of, or for any errors or omissions, the information contained in this book. The adoption and application of the information in this book is at the reader's direction and is his or her sole responsibility.

Change Management The Essentials:
The modern playbook for new and experienced practitioners

Social Media: #changeessentials

Author: Lena Ross

ISBN: 978-1-922337-93-1 (paperback)
978-1-922337-42-9 (ebook)

Cover Design: Amelia Lazarus

Photographer: Charlotte Crompton

Typesetting: Green Hill Publishing

CONTENTS

FOREWORD

Earlier this year, I formalised my collaborations with Lena to create a new company, the Agile Change Leadership Institute. By the time you finish reading this book you will understand why. The decision to do so was a no-brainer - she is generous, creative and so focused on delivering value. And those three hallmarks of Lena's working style shine through in this book.

This book is such an important contribution to the change community (and to be fair, the business sector in general). Despite every new management fad and framework hitting our desks, the need to support people through change remains enduring. It doesn't go away with design thinking, it doesn't go away with new neuroleadership approaches, and it doesn't go away with agile ways of working.

Some might argue it gets harder... and so, the value of a book like this increases. The book is clear, pragmatic, helpful, and abundant with tips of lived experience.

And whether it's the financial lure of the how change practitioners are compensated, or whether it is a core calling to make life better for humans at work, more and more people are coming into the industry seeking to be effective at introducing and supporting others through change. And to my knowledge, up to this point there is NO all-encompassing agnostic handbook that helps you as some-one new to the industry. So the value of this book is immense.

For those who are well established, let me tell you that as an experienced practitioner, in reading this book I had a few wake-up calls and reminders on things I had let lapse in some initiatives. Don't kid yourself it's only for the newbies. It's the type of book you keep close to hand and pick up, check a chapter, put it back, and revisit when your change life gets gnarly again.

This is a book of education, reassurance, support and order in a world that is often ill-informed, hostile, conflict-filled and chaotic. Keep it close by.

Dr Jen Frahm
Conversations of Change
Agile Change Leadership Institute

FIRST THINGS FIRST

PREFACE

A few years ago my daughter, Justine, was completing her last year of secondary school. In Australia, a big part of this final year involves the student scanning the available tertiary courses and degrees to identify what they would like to study post-school and to formally submit their 'preferences'. As a parent who was always interested in her education and aspirations, I went along with her to visit the school careers advisor.

Now, as someone interested in human behaviour, Justine indicated that, among other things, she may be interested in a career in change management. The careers advisor, who was unaware of my occupation, bluntly and emphatically told her that there would be no need for change consultants in five years. It would be a redundant role, she explained, as leaders will be able to do 'change management' as part of their jobs.

Yet here we are a decade later, and change practitioners are still very much in demand across all industries in both permanent and contract roles in most, if not all, of the Western world. There are numerous factors contributing to this demand - the main one being that change is continuous. And it doesn't look as if it's going to diminish any time soon.

To this day, I'm not sure where the careers advisor had sourced her information, nor did I ask at the time. I do know that the role of the change consultant is changing and evolving to meet the demands of a business landscape that is becoming increasingly uncertain and complex. Leaders continue to rely on change professionals to support and advise on change initiatives. There is an increasing recognition that change capability, across all parts of organisations, will improve change resilience and build change maturity overall as a sustainable competitive advantage. There will continue to be a place in organisations for change professionals.

So, future and current change professionals, the outlook is good! If you have an adaptive mindset with endless curiosity and courage to experiment, the brave new world awaits you.

1

INTRODUCTION

In recent decades, organisations have faced unprecedented changes created by technological, social and economic forces. To remain commercially viable, organisations need to be resilient and adaptive. So, too, do the occupations and industries that help these organisations navigate the change. Where challenge meets opportunity, this is the very nature of our role as change consultants. We ourselves need to celebrate and embrace the change that continues to evolve our practice.

Despite the amount of attention on the need for capability in science, technology, engineering and maths (also abbreviated to STEM) to prepare for artificial intelligence (AI) and big data, human-centred skills will continue to be highly valued. While people continue to work in organisations, the foibles and emotions that come with being human will not disappear, nor will the demand for expertise to support people through relentless change.

WHY I WROTE THIS BOOK

This book is written for the *modern* change practitioner - *future* and *present*.

It's for the *future* practitioner because some of you may be thinking about getting into change management and looking to find out as much as you can. And it's for the *present* practitioner because even when you are a seasoned professional, there is always something new to learn, revisit, or share with your team.

Modern? Ah, I was hoping you'd ask that! Because change is changing, we need to adapt and evolve. Practices and tools that served change managers well for so long may not be the ones we need now. In any field, a modern practitioner is one who is not fixed to a specific process, view or methodology and is adaptive in mindset and practice.

The art and science of change management is too diverse and sophisticated to rely on a single toolkit Despite demand, there is a need to continually refresh our capabilities so we can stay relevant and continue to add value. We owe this to:

- our clients
- our industry and peers, and
- ourselves.

One of my frequently asked questions goes like this:

- *How do I get started in change management - what course should I do or what information do I need?*

Sometimes I am surprised at how little emerging or new change practitioners know about the discipline. But I also acknowledge that with so much information out there, it can be overwhelming. So it can be difficult to know where to start, what book to pick up first, what really needs to be known, and what is just 'spin'.

Many paths lead to change. Prospective change practitioners come from many disciplines, so there is no single answer to what one must do to prepare for a career in change management. The practice is multi-disciplinary, so it attracts people from a diverse range of professional backgrounds. It's an exciting role because you have the opportunity to liaise with a wide range of stakeholders across an organisation. Very few roles offer this exposure to diverse business areas.

WHY THIS BOOK IS DIFFERENT

It's practical

This book is not just about theory. It's about how the theory and what they teach you in business schools translates to real practice. It provides proven templates and tables that have been used over and over again. And it's practical enough to equip you with what you need to kick off a change plan and other key deliverables expected of a change manager. The biggest challenge in writing this book is that it cannot possibly cover *every* change management framework, model or practice. It does, however, cover enough to warrant the title 'the essentials'.

It's visual

As a visual person, I look for ways to design my documents with tables and diagrams to make them easier to understand. This book features numerous tables, templates and diagrams, so you can find relevant content and use it over and over again as a valuable go-to resource.

When you see this symbol, it's indicating a small snippet of information that is **good to know**:

For example, it's good to know that throughout this book the terms *change managers, change practitioners* and *change consultants* mean the same thing.

It's contemporary

This book is designed to prepare you for new ways of working - an area which I explain in more detail later. With a future-forward view, it covers the capabilities required of change practitioners in an agile and disruptive environment along with the traditional, core competencies.

It's a guidebook for social media posts

One of the emerging capabilities for change practitioners explored later in the book is the confidence to communicate through various digital channels, including enterprise social networks. We also learn a great deal from industry peers by sharing information and experiences on social media

When you see this hashtag at the end of each chapter, you'll find examples of what you can post on your favourite social media channels. Remember to add **#changeessentials** so I can easily find it and re-share it. This book makes it easy for you!

IT'S YOUR PLAYBOOK!

Most chapters are written so you can read them on their own. Some will be considerably shorter than others. They may not appear in an order that works for you right now, or in the order you may want to consume the information. That's okay. Look at the contents page and see what you'd like to find out more about.

You'll see the book is in five parts:

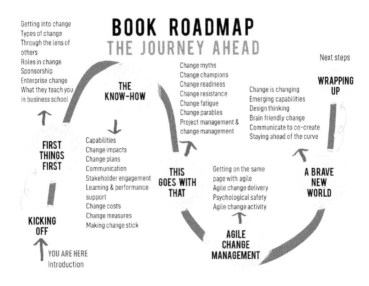

Part One: First things first. To kick off your exploration of change management essentials, we begin with getting into change management, perspectives from new practitioners, and some typical situations you will encounter in organisations. In this section we also look at well-known change models and theories, and how they translate to real-life change activity in practice.

Part Two: The know-how. This section deep dives into core change management capabilities, such as impact assessments, communications and training. It's the nitty-gritty to help you make it happen, with templates and tips on how to kick off your change planning and activities.

Part Three: This goes with that. Along with change management come complementary and support roles such as sponsors, project managers and change champions, as well as myths and parables, and human responses such as resistance and fatigue. This is where these change-related topics are covered.

Part Four: Agile change management. An understanding of how agile practices integrate with change activity will help you quickly play a key role in delivering agile change in all types of projects. This section provides underpinning knowledge on agile change and how to deliver change in fast-moving, agile environments.

Part Five: A brave new world. In this section you will find information on why and how change is changing, and how the role of the change practitioner is evolving to meet these shifts.

At the end of most chapters is a short note that references relevant chapters. Right at the end of the book you will find references, suggested further reading, where to find clips to watch, and a glossary of commonly used change management terms.

Treat this as your change playbook - the one you keep going back to. Make notes in it, attach post-it notes to pages. Do whatever works best for your learning style. Whatever you do, don't lend it to anyone because it's unlikely you'll get it back ☺

RELATED CHAPTERS: All of them!

Where challenge meets opportunity, this is the very nature of our role as change consultants. #changeessentials

#

The art and science of change management is too diverse and sophisticated to rely on a single toolkit. #changeessentials

All about people

2

GETTING INTO CHANGE MANAGEMENT

As mentioned in the last chapter, many paths lead to change. Let's kick off with an industry-wide accepted definition of what change management is.

Prosci[1] defines it as *the discipline that guides how we prepare, equip and support individuals to successfully adopt change in order to drive organizational success and outcomes.*

The change practitioner advises, influences or is consulted on introducing and embedding the change. Their role is to ensure that the impacted people are ready to adopt the new ways.

The types of organisational change are diverse, and definitions of success vary across businesses. The discipline of change management therefore draws on a broad range of skills and expertise to manage and deliver the change. It's no surprise that change practitioners come from diverse disciplines. There is no single prescription for what one must do to prepare for a career in change management. The practice is multi-disciplinary.

---

1 Prosci is an organisation that carries out comprehensive research into change management best practice and provides services to build change capability.

Here's where many change practitioners come from, in no particular order or hierarchy:

- Learning and development
- Communications
- Human resources
- Psychology/behavioural science
- Project management including PMO
- Business analysis
- Engineering
- Graduate rotations
- Experience as a subject matter expert or change champion on a project.

As with any role, career preparation begins with finding out as much as you can about the industry. To help you along, in this book we look at the required capabilities, emerging trends, what change people need to know, types of change, how change itself is changing, where to find the information, and so much more. In other words, reading this book is a fine start!

THE GOLDEN ALIGNMENT

The old 'Catch 22' of getting into a new industry is that you need experience, but how do you get experience in the first place? In occupations that do not have specific vocational training, attending a course or gaining a certification is not enough. So how do you gain the relevant experience to position yourself as someone who is ready to jump into change management?

The pathways or approaches to get into change management are what I call the *golden alignment*. Here's a couple of examples:

Chelsea

A young lady I coached was in her first job after completing an undergraduate business degree. Let's call her Chelsea. Chelsea was enjoying her first year as a Project Management Office (PMO) Analyst working in a large organisation. As she was keen to get into change management, we looked at the activities in her current PMO role to see which responsibilities were aligned to the capabilities of a change practitioner. There was stakeholder management, running meetings and maintaining a visual project management board.

To further build capabilities that align with change management, Chelsea looked for opportunities within her current role. She volunteered to kick off a quarterly project newsletter (communication skills), and to train new team members joining the project, which included developing a new starter's checklist and quick reference guides (learning and performance support skills). Along with building her confidence, this gave Chelsea some real examples to mention in her resume and to talk about in interviews, with artefacts to show. She also scored glowing references from her employer and stakeholders, as she was creating value and demonstrating fabulous initiative.

Another way is to look for an existing change initiative in your company and offer to help.

Andrew

This is exactly what happened to Andrew when his employer was in the process of an acquisition. The employees in his current organisation were all to be 'transitioned' to a new employer and would be required to adopt their systems, move offices and integrate with their new colleagues. Seeing an opportunity, Andrew first discussed his interest with his team leader, who applauded his interest in supporting the change effort. With the endorsement from his leader, Andrew met with the Project Manager to register his interest. He was quickly connected with the Change Management Lead (an external consultant), who was happy to have someone with business knowledge on her side to help. His first task was to help develop the Business Readiness Checklist for 'transition day'. He even managed to get a little change mentoring as well.

Look for the opportunities in your current role which will help you create the golden alignment. The more you know about the capabilities required of a change practitioner, and the types of activity they carry out in their roles, the better equipped you will be to create your own golden alignment so you're job ready!

With the volume of change taking place, look out for these types of pathways to gain relevant experience. As with anything new, at first it may feel uncomfortable. But by stretching yourself outside your comfort zone and beyond the requirements of your current role, you are demonstrating a learning mindset and resilience - things to talk about in your job interview.

RESUME ALIGNMENT

Remember to align your resume to change-related capabilities. Make sure it has a section for *Key Skills*. In that section, include skills that are relevant to change management, with a brief explanation of what you have gained experience in, or what artefacts you have completed.

Here's an example on how to hit the mark:

RESUME
KEY SKILLS EXAMPLE
RESUME: CHELSEA CAMPBELL

KEY SKILLS

COMMUNICATIONS

Develop quarterly project newsletter for distribution to internal and external stakeholders. Maintain project SharePoint site and visual management board.

STAKEHOLDER ENGAGEMENT

Plan and participate in stakeholder engagement forums, e.g. town hall meetings, showcase forums, project control committee meetings.

LEARNING & DEVELOPMENT

Create and update new starter's checklist and provide induction training for new starters. Prepare quick reference guides for new learners.

💡 GOOD TO KNOW

The best approach in your resume is to keep the language simple, and explain any acronyms you use. Look for opportunities to align the language with words in the job advert or role description.

TERMINOLOGY

Don't be baffled by terminology. Consistency in language in the change management profession across organisations and globally is not an exact science.

For example, a *change agent* in one organisation may mean a *change manager*, whilst in another business, it means a *champion of change*. Variation in terminology can confuse not only the change consultants who work across different organisations, but also the people within the business who will be impacted by the change.

Be comfortable with your own understanding of a change practitioner to help you get past varied definitions across organisations and countries.

💡 GOOD TO KNOW

You may hear change referred to as the 'delta'. For example, someone may say to you, 'What's the delta?' If you haven't heard this term before, it's quite confusing. Delta, the fourth letter of the Greek alphabet, is represented as a triangle, like this: $\triangle$. It's also the mathematical symbol for 'variation', as is now sometimes used to mean the word 'change'. You might even see 'change' abbreviated to the triangle, eg $\triangle$ management.

RELATED CHAPTERS: Change capabilities

The discipline of change management draws on a broad range of skills and expertise to manage and deliver the change. #changeessentials

There is no single prescription for what someone must do to prepare themselves for a career in change management. The practice is multi-disciplinary. #changeessentials

3

TYPES OF CHANGE

Project initiatives are often categorised according to the type of change they plan to deliver. Like change management role titles, the terminology used can vary across organisations and industries. Business management textbooks will offer different definitions as well. This inconsistency in labelling types of change confuses people new to the industry. An experienced practitioner who moves across organisations to carry out their work will also see a range of descriptors.

You will pick up strong clues by listening to your project sponsor and project manager. Documentation, such as the Business Case, should reveal nuances of the language and terminology used in that particular organisation. If you're still unsure, it's best to clarify with your project team members.

It's worth noting that change types are not mutually exclusive. For example, a change in office building location may also require culture change to new ways of working. Regardless of how the change is labelled, remember that organisations are made up of people, and people will be impacted by change initiatives, so every type of change is a *people-related* one.

Here are some common change types:

CULTURAL CHANGE

This may be labelled as *strategic change* or *organisation-wide change*.

Cultural change often signals a shift in the organisation's strategic objectives, with a plan to establish new or different business models, behaviours and business objectives. It is one of the most people-centric types of change, as it requires a shift in attitudes and behaviours. For this reason, unlike many other change types, cultural change doesn't have a 'go-live' date where a switch occurs. Shifts in working habits and behavioural norms take some time to become the new 'way we do things around here'.

In recent times, this has become a more common type of change as organisations move to agile or new ways of working. To shape a different work environment, you need to address more than capabilities in your change plan. This type of change relies more than others on WILL as well as SKILL. To signal new ways, organisations often remove artefacts of the old culture, for example, by burning or disposing of old manuals and photographs.

ORGANISATIONAL CHANGE

Restructures are usually referred to as *structural change* or *organisational change*. You can see how some terms may confuse: the term 'organisational change' is also used to broadly define the role of the change practitioner or the change discipline, which is also known as Organisational Change Management (OCM). The reason for an organisational restructure may be:

- A merger or acquisition
- Cost cutting, which often means a reduction in employee head count
- A new business operating model that moves people into different parts of the organisation or into different roles
- Culture change that creates new roles, requiring recruitment of people with aligned skills and mindset.

This is a difficult type of change to manage. as impacted employees may lose their jobs or be reassigned to other roles with little or no choice. When structural changes are taking place, team members may be 're-pointed' to work in a different team or business unit, often with a new manager. When redundancies are involved, there may be engagement with trade unions, usually with the guidance and support of Human Resources team members who are skilled in Industrial Relations. With redundancies comes the need to provide services such as transition support, outplacement, and re-skilling opportunities. Emotional support should be provided in the form of employee assistance programs.

It may not only be the impacted employees who seek emotional support. Often forgotten are the ones left behind - the survivors of the restructures and redundancies. Their immediate response is usually relief, but when they start to understand the scope of the impact, and how their team members and colleagues are affected, they may experience additional stress and what is known as 'survivor guilt' or 'survivor syndrome'. The negative effects on the survivors may be lower morale, higher stress levels and absenteeism, as they may feel their workload will increase when head count is reduced.

In my experience, the survivors are not considered in this type of change. They feel poorly equipped to support their impacted colleagues, while wondering about when the uncertainty and further changes may affect them.

🔆 GOOD TO KNOW

It's worth noting that the work can take an emotional toll on change practitioners engaged on organisational change programs, particularly where redundancies are involved. Be mindful of how the emotional responses of others may impact you, so you can take good care of yourself. Self-care is essential!

TECHNOLOGY IMPLEMENTATIONS/SYSTEM CHANGE

Technological change includes the introduction of new systems or the upgrading of existing ones. It can involve different ways to collect, store and distribute information. The implementation of new hardware or software (or both) is complex, as it almost always impacts upstream and downstream systems, applications and databases.

This type of project and change planning will usually follow the Software Development Life Cycle (SDLC) process to build software, which includes project phases dedicated to the design, development and testing of software solutions before a designated implementation date.

This type of change involves technology training so users are familiar with the new operations and processes. It will often need consideration for post-implementation performance support in a period known as *hyper-care*. This is a phase where users already familiar with the new system (*super users*) are available to help others adopt and become comfortable with the technology change.

BUILDING RELOCATIONS

Moving office, or even an office refurbishment, relies on careful logistics management to help people feel comfortable and enabled from day one. Moving house is ranked to be a very stressful personal event, so moving office is likely to result in some work-related stress. If the move is geographically significant, where the new location is some distance from the existing one, people will be concerned about commuting times and transport to and from work. Some will be excited that the new office is closer to home, while others will resent the additional travel time.

Consideration needs to be given to how different teams or functions will interact with space. For example, a call centre is often located away from other teams in a dedicated area, and may require less open space due to the volume of phone calls and the nature of the work.

In recent times, a new workspace has often equated to a new way of working in an open space environment. A change of environment can represent a change in layout, such as removal of private offices, allocated car parking spaces or designated desks. And often it's not just about space - it's about how people interact with potential new technology and with each other. For the transition to be successful, a building relocation requires a shift in mindset and behaviours. Change managers often recommend visits to the new work location ahead of the move to help employees visualise their future work space. Welcome packs on day one add a personal touch, too.

DIGITAL TRANSFORMATION

You find out you are working on a *digital transformation*. This is an exciting change that is likely to involve a number of changes to areas such as customer products and services, technology and systems, culture and process changes. In order to improve processes, which in turn will improve the customer, vendor and employee experience, digital transformation can involve many types of technology such as workplace collaboration tools, workplace analytics, cloud computing, artificial intelligence (AI), machine learning and robotics.

If a business is to remain competitive and relevant, digital transformation is an imperative, so this type of change is becoming increasingly common.

In digital transformation, the executive sponsor is likely to be the CEO or the Chief Information Officer (CIO).

POLICY CHANGE

A workplace policy ensures consistency by providing a framework, direction and defined responsibilities on workplace standard operating procedures. It clarifies expectations on what employees should do and how they should behave.

You will be familiar with workplace policies, as they form most of the on-boarding compliance training and induction material we receive as new starters. Some examples of recent policy changes in the workplace are around use of personal devices, social media, Casual Fridays, dress codes, recruitment, health and safety, bullying and harassment, diversity and inclusion, annual leave and work/life balance, working remotely, and code of conduct.

Policy change usually impacts all employees and needs careful communication to ensure that all employees understand what is required of them. As policy changes are often linked to compliance, mandatory learning activities will form part of the change planning. For example, all impacted employees may need to complete eLearning modules by a certain date.

Typically, the Human Resources team is the custodian of workplace policies.

PROCESS CHANGE

A change in workflow is characterised by re-engineered processes with the intent to improve efficiencies and productivity.

We are seeing more of this type of change with the introduction of AI and robotics. When the introduction of a new process frees up a great deal of time for employees, there is an expectation that their day-to-day roles will be redefined. Often, this presents an opportunity to upskill and engage in more rewarding work, which results in redefining job descriptions.

For *process change*, it's helpful to clearly communicate what will remain the same and what will change. Send messages about what is robust and positive about current processes so that people feel they are continuing to add value. Sometimes it's not an entirely new process, but simply a refreshed application of an existing one.

PRODUCT DEVELOPMENT

A change in your product or service will almost certainly impact your external customer, who will become a key stakeholder.

These changes may involve different ways in which your customers interact with your products and services. An example is a refreshed internet site where customers are encouraged to self-serve more and interact with online chat bots (AI) rather than call someone for support. When the customer experience changes, it can include direct engagement with external customers or their advocates.

 GOOD TO KNOW

Drivers of change: Each type of change initiative usually occurs for a specific reason, which is often caused by activity in the external business environment. This table shows the typical drivers (apart from what may result from the arrival of a new CEO) for each change type:

Change type	Driver
Cultural	Organisational values realignment, market positioning and image, response to bad publicity
Organisational	Merger and/or acquisition, cost, organisational restructure/realignment
Technology implementation	Relevance, innovation, customer experience
Building relocation	Cost, lease expiry, shifts in employee numbers
Digital transformation	Relevance, innovation, customer experience
Policy change	Legislation, Trade Union negotiations
Process change	Efficiency, effectiveness, business improvement
Product development	Innovation, competitor activity, customer expectation

💡 GOOD TO KNOW

You may hear the term *BaU change* or *Business as Usual change*, as opposed to change initiatives that are delivered by a dedicated project team. BaU change is change that occurs within business units frequently and usually on a small scale, as part of their operations. This type of change is managed by the business, most often without additional or dedicated change practitioners. It may involve a process change or the introduction of new policy. For example, the introduction of 'working from home' policies or guidelines is a BaU change delivered by the Human Resources team. It would typically involve organisational communications, talking points for managers and ensuring that the policy, Frequently Asked Questions and a point of contact are available on the company intranet.

💡 GOOD TO KNOW – YES ANOTHER ONE!

Here's another couple of terms you will meet. You will probably hear the words *change* and *transformation* used interchangeably. Most times, you can let it pass. But a time may come when you need to call it out, or you are asked about the differences. The following short and widely accepted explanation is good to know:

Transformation is explained using the metaphor of a caterpillar emerging as a butterfly over time. The end state (the butterfly) is noticeably different to the initial state (the caterpillar, or even the cocoon). When something completely new emerges, this is transformation.

Change, in contrast, is a series of incremental alterations or improvements that occur while many other things remain the same. If we apply the same metaphor of the caterpillar and butterfly, change would result in an improved or different version of the caterpillar.

It's not surprising that organisational transformation takes longer to achieve, and needs a new operating model and organisational design to result in an end state that is completely different.

RELATED CHAPTERS: Enterprise change management,
project management and change management, change champions.

Regardless of how a change is labelled, we need to remember
that organisations are made up of people, and people will
be impacted by change initiatives, so every type of change is
people-related. #changeessentials

You will probably hear the words *change* and *transformation*
used interchangeably. Most times, you can let it pass. But a
time may come when you need to call it out, or you are asked
about the differences. #changeessentials

THROUGH THE LENS OF OTHERS

You have probably noticed that I'm a big fan of self-directed learning and networking to stay ahead of industry trends. The change practitioners who accelerate in their careers are consistently those who demonstrate a growth mindset with a voracious appetite to learn and experiment.

KEEPING IT REAL

At the end of 2018, our Change Management Institute (CMI) chapter here in Victoria, Australia, recognised outstanding contributors to change management with the inaugural Change Kudos Awards, voted by industry peers. One of the five award categories was 'Newcomer', for the most promising newbie. I'm fortunate to know the winner of the Newcomer category, Daniel Paulet. We worked closely together in one of Australia's largest banks just before Dan kicked off his career in change in another large organisation. One of the key themes in Dan's award nominations was his eagerness to learn, his capacity and commitment to drive his own learning, and the way he generously shares his experiences to help others.

With Dan's permission, I am reprinting here two of his LinkedIn articles, posted two years apart, that attracted a great deal of attention and engagement.

WANT TO START A CAREER IN CHANGE MANAGEMENT?
by Dan Paulet
Posted on LinkedIn on 9 February 2017

··

Trying to work out if a career in Change is right for you? Heard of 'Change Management' and not sure how to make the move? Over the last 12 months, I made a career transition into Change Management. For those that want to take the leap, in this article I will share a little bit about my experience and some of my tips based on what I have learnt so far.

But first, what was my motivation to get into Change? As a line manager, I was continually handed organisational change to roll out to my team, but frequently not supported to embed the change before another change was required to be rolled out. Sound familiar? We can all recall examples of poor organisational change, but it meant the benefits of the change were often not realised and for me, as a line manager, I was frustrated. I decided to take action. I felt I could apply what I had learnt from previous roles and apply it to support organisational change.

For me, change management is about supporting managers to lead their teams through change, building change capability while also helping people understand themselves more in order to recognise why they react to change the way they do.

So I found my motivation to begin a career in change. Now the next challenging step was: how to make my next role align more closely to a change practitioner? With experience not directly aligned to Change Management, I began to look at job ads to understand experience and qualifications that were required for change roles. A major requirement in the Job ads were Organisational Change Management certifications. After some deliberation, I decided on completing a Prosci Change Management qualification. I found that by attending the course, it solidified what I understood as Change Management and provided me with a framework that I could talk to for job interviews and networking conversations.

Ah yes, I am here, networking! Networking with purpose, which I made easier by being clear on my motivation, and having an understanding of a change management framework.

This gave me the opportunity to be able to focus on where I could provide value (both in networking conversations and interviews).

Since starting a role as a change practitioner, I have been supporting transformational change in a global company. Has it been what I expected? From a change activities perspective, absolutely, and adapting those activities so they are fit for purpose. From a soft skills perspective, I have been flexing my active listening muscles more than ever. Being tuned into what is being said, and what isn't. And I am learning something new every day.

These are my top five tips for new starters interested in careers in Change Management based on what I have learnt so far.

1. KNOW YOUR WHY.

Yes I know I am channelling Simon Sinek here, but it is important to be clear on your motivation - whether it's in Change, or any other career. Does it align to the work you enjoy doing? Some of the online tools that helped me understand myself a bit more were the VIA character strengths survey and the 16 personalities Myer's Briggs test.

2. EMBRACE YOUR LEARNING MINDSET.

Be comfortable with where you are in your own development. As I mentioned earlier, I completed a Prosci Change Management accreditation; while it has absolutely given me a solid foundation on which I can grow my Change career, it is another tool in the toolkit to support organisational change. I am quickly learning change is not lineal (as it is in the textbook) and a number of tools may be required to support the change to being successful.

3. UNDERSTAND PROJECT MANAGEMENT.

Since starting in a change role, I have found that having a background in and around project delivery has been beneficial. Being able to speak the same language as project management colleagues and align change deliverables has increased the visibility and the important role that change has to play in the project.

4. BE ADAPTABLE, OPEN TO AMBIGUITY YET REMAIN FOCUSED.

While ambiguity often goes hand in hand with organisational change, the reality is that as people are experiencing change differently (and what it means for them), you may be caught up in office politics. Consider what tools you may have to support, while being focused on the long-term prize of successful change delivery.

5. BE AUTHENTIC.

I am learning that not every problem needs a solution straight away. Don't be afraid to say, "This is going to need a bit more thinking". A quick response to a stakeholder may not be to consider the bigger picture of the change that is being delivered. Oh and it goes a long way too with developing your relationships and managing stakeholder expectations (yep that old chestnut).

A CAREER IN CHANGE MANAGEMENT – THE RIDE SO FAR...
by Dan Paulet
Posted on LinkedIn on 24 February 2019

A few years ago I made a shift into a career in Change Management. I shared my experiences in starting a career in Change Management in my article 'Want to start a career in Change Management?' Now, with experience in the field, I am often asked my learnings. This article focuses on just a few of the top things that I have learnt.

Firstly, let's get this out on the table straight away: Change Management is not for the faint of heart. Humans are complex, each with their own motivators, desires, values and goals – yes we are all unique snowflakes. Change Management is more than just a toolkit (insert your favourite Change methodology), it requires a whole bunch of coaching, listening, strategic positioning, navigating tough conversations and that might all be before your morning coffee. So agility, adaptability and resilience are key to surviving a role in change.

What else have I learnt? Here's the top five!

1) **Blend your Business Impact Assessments.**

   I have had some great results using Human Centred Design approaches to journey mapping with business stakeholders to understand their current state environment. It helps to identify if there are underlying issues within the environment be it process, systems or team. Getting a deeper understanding of their pain/ gain points in their current journey can also start to help build your benefits profile if they align to what your project is delivering (great for selling the dream). I completed an online course via IDEO on Human Centred Design with some likeminded Change professionals to add to my tool kit. Lena Ross also speaks about Human Centred Design approaches in her Hacking for Agile Change book, which I would highly recommend as a read for budding Change Practitioners.

2) **Communication plans work. Fact.**

   There is nothing worse than getting that email that something new is about to start, a day before a business change happens. It's 2019, we are better than that! Unfortunately, it still happens. I have found that even a simple plan is better than nothing. We know through ADKAR we need to create awareness and desire for the change. Build your strategy and work closely with your leaders to help them understand their role in communication, and more importantly the potential impacts of deviation from the plan. Consider how your message may need to be adapted if a component of engagement is missed. Refer to earlier point on agility ;).

3) **Throw out all the buzzwords.**

When the watercooler starts bubbling out these buzzwords, it's time to shake things up. Use simple language; where possible avoid jargon. It goes a long way in building trust and confidence with a business. In one of my roles I had a cheeky way to influence behavioural change within the project team. The creation of the 'Journey Jar'. Similar to a swear jar, anytime someone said journey, $1 was to be donated to the jar. It really made the team conscious of the language we were using and it was fun and the language became much more action-orientated. Rather than taking people on the journey, we would engage, listen and deliver.

4) **Measure it!**

Spend time on understanding the success metrics of the change. And like they always say, make them realistic. Additional to surveys you can track engagement in a variety of ways including new threads of conversation on your company social media platform, attendance to project briefings, views on intranet articles/pages etc. When building your metrics, success might look different for different teams or companies depending on their change maturity. For me, I have found that tracking the change success was a good way to keep my finger on the pulse and, where intervention was required, I could quickly adjust the plan to bring it back on course.

5) **I do; engagement.**

We have lots of different ways to engage people within a business, yet we often default to a Skype briefing whether it be due to time or location-based constraints. But let me tell you, face-to-face engagement wins hands down every time.

Try this one next time for your Skype Briefing. Set up a poll before the session and release it midway through the session. Try the same poll when your change leader is in front of an audience. What is the result? Chances are that person who is in your Skype briefing is sending off that 'urgent' email and has missed all the key messages. I have also found that keeping your engagement sessions short and sharp build a whole bunch more respect from the business stakeholders.

The above is just some of the learnings since I have started working as a Change Practitioner. Of course, all good learnings come with a good story and I will continue to share my experiences in this year's #changeblogchallenge.

I couldn't finish this article without a shout out to some of the amazing Change professionals I have had the pleasure to work with, learn with and most importantly laugh with over the last few years as I have kicked off this career in Change Management

Jennifer Frahm, Joanne King and Stacy Payne, thank you.

You can follow Dan on LinkedIn

https://www.linkedin.com/in/danielpaulet/

💡 GOOD TO KNOW

You can learn a lot from real stories such as these from the trenches, as opposed to change management text books. Keep an eye out for similar LinkedIn posts where new, emerging and experienced change practitioners, such as Dan Paulet, share their experiences.

Don't restrict your search to articles. Look out for conversations that have been started in LinkedIn Groups such as Organizational Change Practitioners, Association of Change Management Professionals (ACMP) and Change Management Institute (CMI), where the dialogue is rich in advice, experience, and sometimes controversy to spark your curiosity!

💡 GOOD TO KNOW

In 2019, Dr Jen Frahm from Conversations of Change, along with Heather Stagl from Enclaria, kicked off the *#changeblogchallenge* - a call to action to all change aficionados to share their wisdom and expertise throughout 2019, in blogs on four nominated themes, one for each quarter. The themes were resistance, communication, change readiness and change leadership. Do a content search on LinkedIn for *#changeblogchallenge* to read the amazing contributions from around the globe.

5

ROLES IN CHANGE MANAGEMENT

It can be easy to confuse the notion of roles in change management. The terminology used to describe change-related roles is not consistent.

LOOK BEYOND THE JOB TITLE

When you are looking at change management job adverts, look beyond the role title. It's more important to closely review the work that is required, the expected deliverables, and the scale and scope of the project or initiative.

Role titles will vary across organisations, industries and even geographically. Sometimes they may vary within the same company. They will also be adapted to the role being carried out. For example, if you are working on a small project you may be the *change lead*, and on your next assignment which is a larger program of work, your designated role could be *change analyst*. A title often represents context, as well as the scope and scale of the project - it's relative rather than absolute.

The more you know about the common types of change initiatives and the core change capabilities, the better you will be able to decode the job adverts.

For a change practitioner, a job advert may ask for:

- Change analyst
- Change agent
- Senior change analyst
- Change manager
- Change lead
- Senior change manager
- Change consultant
- Business readiness lead
- Implementation specialist
- Change advisor
- Transformation consultant
- Transformation lead
- Change enablement manager
- Change adoption advisor
- Business transition manager
- Organisational Change Management (OCM) Consultant
- Organisational Design Specialist
- Change and Communications Manager
- Change and Training Manager
- Organisational Development Lead
- Program change manager
- Director of Change, Head of Change.

This list is not exhaustive, and many more variations can be found and will continue to appear.

EARLY CAREER AND STARTING OUT

When you are starting out in change management, don't be bamboozled by these titles. Instead, look for opportunities to join a team of change practitioners in a larger organisation or project. You will learn as much by observing as you will by supporting the change activity.

THE LARGE ORGANISATION

Most large organisations employ change professionals as permanent employees, along with contract or fixed-term consultants to meet fluctuations in project demand. Where there is an established *Enterprise Change Management Office* or *Change Practice*, you will often find a clearer career path with defined capabilities for each role in the change job family. A *job family* is a group of jobs related by common skills, knowledge and capabilities.

The change job family typically looks like this:

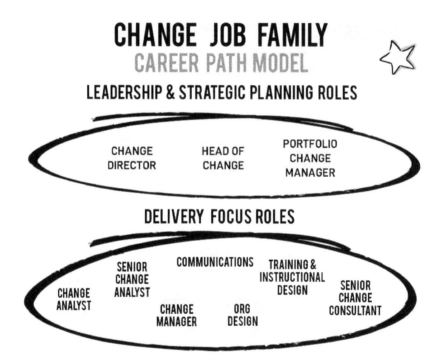

In a large organisation, you will find several 'Heads of Change' who may operate in different business areas, or a Change Director - or both! By contrast, in a smaller organisation, there may be one 'Head of Change' who is the lead change practitioner in that entire business.

CAPABILITY PROFILES

In my experience with establishing Enterprise Change Practices, I've created many change capability profiles and frameworks, particularly for the delivery-focused roles in the change job family. The purpose of a capability framework is to define what is expected in each role while providing a guide for career planning.

A *capability framework* is made up of a list of relevant capabilities for a function or job family. Here's an example of the core capability of Change Communications, representing four levels of expertise:

Change Analyst	Senior Change Analyst	Change Manager	Senior Change Consultant
Contributes to the development of the project communication plan.	*Contributes to developing and executing the project communication plan and/or strategy.* *Develops communication materials to support the readiness, implementation and adoption of the change.*	*Develops, socialises and implements a project communications plan that is targeted to the needs of all impacted stakeholder groups, using a variety of channels.* *Ensures that there is support for, and business ownership of, the implementation of the communication to their teams.* *Monitors and assesses the effectiveness of communications.*	*Oversees the development and execution of a program-wide communication plan that supports all impacted stakeholder groups, using a variety of channels.* *Considers contingency communications and alignment of key messages across multiple projects (other than own project/program) as part of communications plan.*

Change Analyst	Senior Change Analyst	Change Manager	Senior Change Consultant
Communication material, eg emails.	Communications Plan for a *small project.*	Detailed communications schedule and analysis of effectiveness for a *medium to large project.*	*Program level* communications planning, including engagement with Corporate Affairs team.

You can see the incremental capability expected for each role level. When designing a role profile, it's assumed that the employees displaying the capability at a higher profile level in the job family can demonstrate the capabilities and the deliverables listed at the lower profile. This is designed so the descriptions don't repeat themselves.

ON A LARGE CHANGE INITIATIVE

This diagram shows what a change team within a large program of work may look like. In this scenario, the organisation is introducing major system changes that impact all business areas.

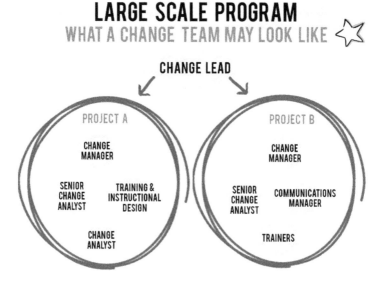

LARGE SCALE PROGRAM
WHAT A CHANGE TEAM MAY LOOK LIKE

CHANGE LEAD

PROJECT A
- CHANGE MANAGER
- SENIOR CHANGE ANALYST
- TRAINING & INSTRUCTIONAL DESIGN
- CHANGE ANALYST

PROJECT B
- CHANGE MANAGER
- SENIOR CHANGE ANALYST
- COMMUNICATIONS MANAGER
- TRAINERS

COMPLEMENTARY ROLES

On a smaller project, the change manager's scope of activity includes communication and training interventions. On larger projects or programs of work, it's not unusual to see roles that are dedicated to communications or training, or both.

Communications specialist

The nature of larger change initiatives may call for a change communications professional. In some organisations the communications specialist works in a matrix environment, reporting to both the program manager or the change lead, and the head of internal communications. This occurs when the project demands a high volume of communications across varied stakeholder groups. For example, some projects communicate regular updates to the company's board of directors and other external stakeholders such as trade unions and vendors.

Training specialist

Some change initiatives with high numbers of impacted users need a great deal of planned training activity and learning collateral to help people build their capability for the new ways in processes, technology, customer interactions and behaviours. Expertise in instructional design and training delivery is valuable for developing quality content that hits the mark, is well-paced and can be handed over to the business after implementation.

A NOTE ON THE 'CHANGE AGENT'

This chapter does not intend to diminish the title of *change agent*, which is not a commonly used term in Australia. The terms *change agent* and *change manager* are often used interchangeably. The *change agent* is sometimes a *change champion*. When you hear the term, it's a good idea to clarify if the intent is to mean 'change manager' or something else.

> ### 💡 GOOD TO KNOW
>
> Look beyond the role title; look for the opportunity!

RELATED CHAPTERS: Enterprise change management, Change capabilities, Project management and change management

It can be easy to confuse the notion of roles in change management. The terminology used to describe change-related roles is not consistent. #changeessentials.

Look beyond the role title; look for the opportunity. #changeessentials.

6

CHANGE SPONSORSHIP

It's no surprise that strong and visible sponsorship and leadership is needed to introduce and embed change in any business or organisation.

Somewhere in the C-Suite, a decision is made to introduce planned change. It may be a cultural transformation, a major system change, an organisational restructure or a digital transformation. A senior executive is appointed, or self-selects, to be the Sponsor of the change program.

The key role of the Project or Change Sponsor is to be the chief advocate for the initiative and to ensure the change delivers the business benefits. Program Managers and Project Managers often report to the sponsor and to a leader in the project management practice.

Sponsors, however, are not all created equal. Most will be committed to the change initiative, but some will be half-hearted or ambivalent, especially if they have been told by a more senior executive that they are sponsoring the change.

The more visible and active your sponsor is, the more likely the change is to land successfully. Ideally, the sponsor will bring together a team of leaders representing the affected business areas in the organisation who will support and guide the change. You will see this group called a *project steering committee, project steering group, project control board* or a *guiding coalition*, among many other names or acronyms. This is the senior stakeholder group.

By the time a change practitioner lands on a project, it's likely the steering committee has been formed. This team answers the following questions to create and provides information for a documented business case or 'case for change':

- Why is the organisation introducing this project or change?
- What is the business imperative? This often includes a narrative on what is taking place in the broader business environment, any regulatory change, changing customer expectations, market forces, competitor activity, and other commercially compelling reasons to respond quickly with organisational change.
- What does the future state look like?
- What changes? What remains the same?
- What are the risks of not implementing the project or change?

THE SPONSOR IS KING

Research consistently confirms that the role of an active and visible sponsor is critical.

Prosci has been carrying out industry research on the people side of change management for 20 years, gathering feedback and insights from thousands of change and project professionals from across the globe. Every two years, Prosci publishes a comprehensive report - the *Best Practices in Change Management Benchmarking Report* - which provides a range of insights including the greatest contributors to change success and obstacles. Their most recent one (at the time of this publication) is the 2018 report in which over 1,750 people from more than 80 countries participated.

Since Prosci commenced their research in 1998, they have found that *the number one contributor to change success is active and visible sponsorship.*

Other factors contributing to success are:
- Dedicated change management resources
- Structured change management approach
- Employee engagement and participation
- Frequent and open communication
- Integration and engagement with project management
- Engagement with middle managers.

Source: Prosci Best Practices in Change Management Benchmarking Report 2018

The importance of the sponsor's role cannot be underestimated:

> Sponsorship has been number one on the list of top contributors in all
> of Prosci's benchmarking reports since 1998. Though much has changed
> in the field of change management over the last two decades, the impor-
> tance of the leader's role in change has remained constant.

Source: Prosci, Executive Sponsor's Importance and Role - Thought Leadership Articles.

DOCUMENTING THE ROLE OF THE SPONSOR

Larger organisations, with well-established Project Centres of Excellence
that maintain project governance, define the role of sponsors and project
teams in documented *Terms of Reference*. These documents outline the
purpose, roles and responsibilities of the sponsors. Logic may tell us that
a senior sponsor shouldn't need this, but if they are new to their sponsorship role, it's helpful to set expectations and monitor standards.

CHARACTERISTICS OF A GOOD SPONSOR

A good sponsor:
- Remains visible and attends key meetings
- Provides clarity around why the change is important
- Is approachable and accessible to project leadership team members
- Models the desired behaviours

- Gains respect from employees not just through positional power, but through their actions
- Makes time to commit to the initiative.

ROLE OF A PROJECT SPONSOR

An active sponsor leads and directs the initiative to:
- Identify opportunities for improvement
- Take timely, corrective action to remove obstacles, escalating to relevant senior stakeholders when needed
- Ensure the program delivers relevant, measurable benefits that support business and organisational objectives
- Ensure stakeholders are effectively engaged and managed across the business
- Adhere to defined governance principles and practices
- Represent the first point of escalation for issues and risks
- Set expectations with project steering committee, managers and team leaders.

Keep in mind that the role of sponsor is additional to their day-to-day responsibilities. When they take on the role of sponsor, it is done with consideration of their existing responsibilities and work load to assess if they have time to effectively support and sponsor the project.

 GOOD TO KNOW

Our role as change practitioners is to support the sponsor's vision and commitment to the change by ensuring that our people are ready to adopt the new ways with the right mindset and skillset.

WHEN SPONSORSHIP IS WEAK OR ABSENT

When sponsorship is not visible, committed or strong, the likelihood of realising the business benefits are compromised. The Program Manager, or Project Manager, who regularly meets with the sponsor will recognise a lack of commitment.

According to Conner Partners, the effects of poorly sponsored change are costly. As with poor leadership, the costs are wasted time, money and human resources, poor morale and low engagement, and a failure to effectively implement the change that was intended to improve business performance.

A while back, I consulted on a project that was in its early phase, with funding approved for the *seeding phase* only. This was the term used in this organisation for investigation and feasibility, before committing to further funding to progress. I worked with the Program Director to prepare a submission to the Program Sponsor for funding to continue the project.

I'm not sure how or why this person was the Program Sponsor in the first place. In hindsight, it was better to find out earlier rather than later that she wasn't committed to the ethos of the project. It was focused on the Employee Experience with Technology, but she told us that she believed she knew what the employees wanted, and a project dedicated to uncover employee problems and insights was no longer required.

SUPPORTING THE SPONSOR

The change plan outlines the activities that will support the sponsor's vision. In your role as a change practitioner, you also directly help sponsors by:

- Suggesting alternative communications channels to promote their visibility, such as enterprise social networks like *Yammer* or *Slack*
- Inviting them to stand-up meetings and engagement events, such as project showcases
- Showing them your project's visual management wall and change plan on a page.

With access to the sponsor, you can demonstrate the nature of the planned change activities and the value they add to promote adoption and acceptance, which in turn translates to benefits realisation.

RELATED CHAPTERS: Change planning

#

Our role as change practitioners is to support the sponsor's vision and commitment to the change by ensuring that our people are ready to adopt the new ways with the right mindset and skillset. #changeessentials.

7

ENTERPRISE CHANGE MANAGEMENT

Just like project management, change management is now recognised as a practice and discipline in its own right. Because of this, more organisations are establishing a 'change management practice' or 'enterprise change management' to co-ordinate and manage change activity within the business.

This term *Enterprise Change Management,* often abbreviated to ECM, is an approach where change management is centralised within an organisation with the objective of delivering change in a consistent and responsive way while lifting change awareness and capability.

PURPOSE OF ENTERPRISE CHANGE MANAGEMENT

Many larger organisations can see the benefits of bringing together what are often fragmented change efforts or numerous change teams from various business units. Establishing an Enterprise Change Management Office acknowledges that change is a discipline with a distinct set of capabilities. It also signals that the organisation is committed to building change management and change leadership as an organisational capability. This is becoming increasingly relevant in a business climate where change is ongoing, rather than a series of discrete events.

This approach is consistent with the complementary disciplines of Project Management and Business Analysis, which often establish their own centres of excellence. Together with Change Management, these disciplines often make up a consolidated group, or business unit, such as *Business Project Services* or *Enterprise Business Transformation*. This book, however, focuses on the change management practice.

ENTERPRISE BUSINESS TRANSFORMATION OFFICE
DISCIPLINES

| PROJECT MANAGEMENT PRACTICE | BUSINESS ANALYSIS PRACTICE | CHANGE MANAGEMENT PRACTICE |

CHARACTERISTICS OF THE ENTERPRISE CHANGE MANAGEMENT OFFICE

While the composition and operations of the Enterprise Change Management Office (ECMO) will vary across organisations, some common characteristics are:

- A name such as ECMO, Change Centre of Excellence or Change Practice
- The application of a standard change management methodology or framework - this can be a framework designed specifically for the organisation or an existing one such as *Prosci* or *People Centred Implementation (PCI)*
- A close working relationship between the ECMO and complementary practices, such as Project Management Office (PMO), Project Management (PM) and Business Analysis (BA), to ensure project and change success

- A commitment to building the capability of the practitioners, such as a Community of Practice
- Encouragement or expectation that work produced and key learnings are shared across the practice to lift the overall capability
- A mechanism that captures changes taking place across the business so there is a common understanding of the volume of change taking place, often expressed visually in a change heat map.

BENEFITS

When an organisation establishes an Enterprise Change Management Office, it will require dedicated and experienced resources such as a Practice Manager or Head of Change Management, along with additional experienced practitioners to support the operation of the ECMO.

In return for this investment in dedicated resources, the organisation can expect to see many benefits as it:

- Removes the duplication of effort of creating commonly used change tools and templates
- Creates a forum for knowledge management with a central knowledge repository
- Signals that change management, as a capability, is valued by the business
- Provides a common language and understanding
- Articulates the change management value proposition
- Increases the likelihood of change practitioner involvement early in the project life cycle
- Defines the change capabilities and offers a clear career path and professional development, improving the employee value proposition
- Enables consolidated change reporting to provide a portfolio and an enterprise view of change initiatives underway to leaders and stakeholders

- Builds a 'pool' of change professionals, leading to efficiencies in resource planning and allocation of change resources to projects
- Creates a sense of community among the change professionals within the business
- Improves the organisation's overall *change maturity*
- Enhances job satisfaction of team members as they are part of a peer community within the organisation.

Establishing and implementing an Enterprise Change Management Office (ECMO) is a change project in itself, requiring planning, engagement and executive sponsorship to set it up for success. It's certainly an exciting time to be working in an organisation when the ECMO is being created. I've been lucky to be involved in the set up in a few organisations and have witnessed the positive energy it creates within and outside the change team.

ENTERPRISE CHANGE MATURITY

Many disciplines have research-based industry-standard maturity models or frameworks to guide continuous improvement and to define occupational goals and standards. Such models may be accompanied by self-assessment questionnaires, or professional audits, to help teams and organisations understand their current state, or level of maturity, and identify a target state.

When a business implements an enterprise focus to build change management as a core organisational capability, it is improving its overall *change maturity*. One key role of the ECMO is to help the organisation become more 'change mature'.

In change management, it is helpful to read maturity models which have been developed by organisations such as Prosci and Change First, as they describe the characteristics of each level of maturity, from no change management to an optimal level of capability across the business.

Referencing an established change maturity model helps organisations define change management best practice; and it provides a roadmap for them to identify opportunities for improvement so they can continue to build their change maturity. Many change practice leaders self-assess their maturity against the definitions of levels offered on checklists such as the one you can find on Change First's website.

Typically, at the lower end of the maturity scale, change management is an isolated process that sometimes occurs in projects in an uncoordinated way. As change management is applied more consistently across the organisation, maturity improves; and along with an understanding of the discipline, a common language and methodology becomes apparent. At the highest levels of maturity, we see change management capability valued, defined and embedded across the organisation.

💡 GOOD TO KNOW

An understanding of change maturity is useful. When you join an organisation, you will be able to quickly gauge the level of change maturity. In turn, it will help you navigate conversations and manage expectations. A recruiter may give you an indication as to whether your client or employer has a good level of change maturity in their business... or not!

RELATED CHAPTERS: Roles in change management

An understanding of change maturity is useful. When you join an organisation, you will be able to quickly gauge the level of change maturity. In turn, it will help you navigate conversations and manage expectations. #changeessentials.

8

WHAT THEY TEACH YOU IN BUSINESS SCHOOL

Having completed an MBA that included two elective units in change management, I can write about this with a high degree of confidence. I've also seen the undergraduate content for many Bachelor of Business degrees.

When you learn about change management at university or in a business school, you will cover *seminal work* on the discipline. This means work that has been highly influential in shaping the concept or subject area through the creation of a new model or theory.

Even though change is changing, an underpinning knowledge of this work, and how the discipline has evolved, helps us understand the first principles which are helpful in navigating complexity.

WHAT THEY SHOULD SPEND MORE TIME ON

What seems to be missing in most academic units on change management is how the theory is applied in organisations. In this chapter, I've added a commentary on how you may see the model used in organisations, or how it is represented in change plans and activity.

Before I briefly explain each one, here's an overview of some the main models or theories that are good to know:

Theme	Researcher/s	Model or Framework
Action Research	Kurt Lewin	Progressive problem solving by active participation
Personal Transition and Loss	Elisabeth Kubler-Ross	Denial, Anger, Bargaining, Depression, Acceptance
	William Bridges	Three transition phases: Ending, losing and letting go; neutral zone; new beginnings
Resistance	Scott and Jaffe	Denial, Resistance, Exploration, Commitment
	Kurt Lewin	Force field analysis
Measuring Attitudes	Rensis Likert	Multi-level Likert Scale: From *Strongly Agree* to *Strongly Disagree*
Building Commitment	Daryl Conner and Robert Patterson	Commitment Curve: Contact, Awareness, Understanding, Positive Perception, Experimentation, Adoption, Institutionalisation, Internalisation
Adoption	Rogers Everett	Diffusion of Innovation (curve)
Planned Change	Kurt Lewin	Unfreeze, change, refreeze
	John Kotter	Eight-step process also known as 'Kotter's 8 steps'
Emotional Intelligence	Daniel Goleman	Self-Awareness, Self-Management, Motivation, Empathy, Social Skills and Awareness

ACTION RESEARCH: KURT LEWIN

Any study of organisational behaviour and change management is not complete without reference to German-American psychologist, Kurt Lewin, who is recognised as one of the founding fathers of social and organisational psychology. In 1944 he developed the concept of *Action Research* - a method of interactive inquiry into an activity or occupation to identify opportunities for improvement.

How it's applied

The purpose of Action Research is to solve a problem with others in a team environment, making it an early approach to managing change through engagement with others.

TRANSITION AND LOSS: ELISABETH KUBLER-ROSS

In 1969 Elisabeth Kubler-Ross, a Swiss-American psychiatrist, developed a model to explain how personal grief is experienced, in the five stages of *denial, anger, bargaining, depression* and *acceptance*. The model appeared in her book *On Death and Dying* to help people understand the emotional states of terminally ill patients after diagnosis, and is often mistakenly associated with loss experienced after death. Whilst there are five stages, Kubler-Ross acknowledges that the process is not always linear and straightforward.

The incorrect association with death and dying has prompted many cynics to question the relevance of Kubler-Ross' model. Interestingly, Daryl Conner (mentioned later in this chapter) investigated this, and in 2012 he described the Kubler-Ross model to be 'just as applicable to the corporate world as it was to the clinical world'. He found the sequencing in the model to be as relevant to people in organisations downsizing as it was to individuals and their family members facing news of terminal illness. It's proven to be a viable model for people experiencing negative or unwelcome change.

How it's applied

Kubler-Ross's model has inspired numerous *change curves* and frameworks, as it acknowledges emotional responses and the need to support people to move through the phases to acceptance.

PERSONAL TRANSITION: WILLIAM BRIDGES

William Bridges, a change consultant, developed a three-phase transition model which features in his book *Managing Transitions*. While change is something that can happen to people or be imposed, Bridges created this model to differentiate personal transition from planned change, with transition as the internal process that is experienced by the change receiver. The three phases are:

1 | Ending, losing and letting go

2 | Neutral phase

3 | New beginnings.

How it's applied

This transition model appears in change plans and slide presentations when change managers are explaining typical human responses to imposed change and how the planned change activity supports impacted users through the phases.

RESISTANCE: SCOTT AND JAFFE

A popular model that explains resistance to change is the *Resistance Cycle*, also known as the *Change Grid*, developed by Cynthia Scott and Dennis Jaffe in 1988. Based on the work of Kubler-Ross, the cycle features four stages that occur across time:

1 | Deny

2 | Resist

3 | Explore

4 | Commit.

How it's applied

This model may appear in change plans and slide presentations to explain resistance.

RESISTANCE AND FORCE FIELD ANALYSIS: KURT LEWIN

As a keen social psychologist, Kurt Lewin also developed the *Force Field Analysis* framework to explore how an issue or plan is affected by external forces. It appeared in 1951 in his book *Field Theory in Social Science*. A line in the middle of the framework represents the equilibrium or the current state, which needs to be disrupted for change to take place. The framework proposes that for change to be successful, we must either maximise the forces for the change or minimise the forces against the change, or both.

How it's applied

The Force Field Analysis drives a productive discussion with your project team members and change champion, to brainstorm the positive forces that will drive or support the change, and the restraining forces that will present obstacles to the change. It opens a conversation on how you can strengthen or leverage the positive forces and minimise or manage the obstacles. The discussion will provide a common understanding of the proposed change and potential resistance, as well as clues on your change interventions or approach; and it uncovers possible risks and issues to identify for your project.

FORCE FIELD ANALYSIS

FORCES FOR CHANGE	FORCES AGAINST CHANGE

DRIVING FORCE 1

RESTRAINING FORCE 1

DRIVING FORCE 2

RESTRAINING FORCE 2

DRIVING FORCE 3

RESTRAINING FORCE 3

RESTRAINING FORCE 4

DRIVING FORCE 4

SOURCE: Framework developed by social psychologist, Kurt Lewin, in the 1950s.

MEASURING ATTITUDES: RENSIS LIKERT

No doubt you've completed a survey or feedback questionnaire that features the *Likert Scale,* named after its inventor, American social psychologist Rensis Likert. It's the most widely used set of options presented to measure the scale of your response or attitude to an issue.

The Likert Scale appears as a set of five, seven, or sometimes nine fixed-choice options that may range from *Strongly Disagree* to *Strongly Agree* to gauge the intensity of the user's experience.

How it's applied

If you need to design surveys forms in your change roles, such as Change Readiness Assessments or Training Evaluations, it's likely that you will use a Likert Scale to measure attitudes.

BUILDING COMMITMENT TO CHANGE: DARYL CONNER AND ROBERT PATTERSON

Daryl Conner is internationally recognised as a change management thought leader. In 1982, with Robert Patterson, he co-authored an article in the *Training and Development Journal* titled 'Building Commitment to Organizational Change'. Also appearing in Conner's 1992 book *Managing at the Speed of Change*, this framework features eight steps to building commitment. It is now widely known as the 'change curve' or 'commit-ment curve', and shows how commitment is built and maintained in stages across time:

1 | Contact

2 | Awareness

3 | Understanding

4 | Positive perception

5 | Experimentation

6 | Adoption

7 | Institutionalization

8 | Internalization.

How it's applied

The eight stages are often simplified to four: *awareness, understanding, positive perception* and *commitment*. The simplified model (also covered in the chapter on *Stakeholder Engagement*) is often used in stakeholder analysis. It's also used in change readiness surveys to identify which stage of commitment the impacted users and stakeholders have reached at a given point in time.

ADOPTION: EVERETT ROGERS

A popular approach to explain adoption is Everett Rogers' *Diffusion of Innovations* model, developed in 1962. Rogers, a Professor of Communication Studies, developed the model to demonstrate the rate at which new ideas and technology spread. He proposes that a new idea needs communication, time, and a social system along with the idea or product itself to gain enough traction to be sustainable, to reach critical mass.

According to Rogers' model, adoption takes place with categories of users defined as *innovators, early adopters, early majority, late majority* and *laggards.*

How it's applied

This model may appear in change plans and slide presentations as a way to explain user adoption. The *innovators* are typically the change initiators. In change efforts, change champions and super users become your *early adopters*, acting as your evangelists to gain support and enable further adoption. Your most resistant users are often referred to as the *laggards.*

PLANNED CHANGE: KURT LEWIN (ALLEGEDLY)

The three-step model of *unfreeze, change* and *refreeze* has been attributed to Kurt Lewin. Whilst there is no evidence that Lewin developed this approach, it is accepted as a key framework in change management. It's often cited to make sense of how to plan for change in a business context, using ice as a metaphor to explain the three steps of unfreeze, change and refreeze.

Imagine you start with a cube of ice that represents the current state. The business decides to introduce a change that will result in a different future state. First you must unfreeze the cube, or current state. In this phase, communicate the vision as part of the unfreeze process. Before shaping the future state, you need to create the new shape during the change phase. During this phase, you help people prepare for the future state through performance support activity such as training, communications and engagement. In the final phase of refreeze, the new shape is created. The new ways have been adopted and this phase concentrates on embedding the change.

How it's applied

This model is often cited to make sense of how to plan for change in a business context, using ice as a metaphor to explain the three steps:

1 | Unfreeze

2 | Change

3 | Refreeze.

PLANNED CHANGE IN STEPS: JOHN KOTTER

Harvard Leadership Professor, John Kotter, introduced his widely known eight-step model for successful change in his 1996 book, *Leading Change*. The absence of these eight steps is often cited as the reason change efforts fail in an organisation.

On the next page is an overview of John Kotter's eight steps and some typical activities that take place during change projects:

Step		Activities
1	**Establish a sense of urgency**	Executives identify a need for the change and the risks of NOT changing.
		Communicate early company announcements
2	**Form a guiding coalition**	Identify a change/project sponsor and a senior steering committee who will work closely with the project team.
3	**Create a vision**	Write the business case with anticipated benefits of the change - qualitative and quantitative.
		Identify what needs to change, eg process, behaviours, capabilities, mindset, technology, space.
		Develop a change plan that includes communications and engagement - identify key messages, to which audience, and when.
4	**Communicate the vision**	Implement the communications and stakeholder engagement plan.
		Enable forums for two-way communication to identify concerns.
5	**Empower others to act on the vision**	Kick off the change champion program and other activities that promote co-creation and buy-in, eg impact assessment workshops, employee journey mapping, change readiness surveys.
6	**Plan for and create short-term wins**	Reward your change advocates.
		Celebrate and communicate your project milestones, eg employee personas and journey maps are complete, change network champions identified and briefed, testing is complete.
7	**Consolidate improvements and produce still more change**	Gather positive user stories about adoption and business benefits.
8	**Embed the new approaches**	Align performance scorecards and metrics to support the new ways.
		Retell stories.
		Ensure leaders are modelling the new behaviours and practices.

How it's applied

In his book *The Heart of Change,* Kotter himself provides a compelling example on how to create a sense of urgency with visual impact. This is known as the 'gloves on the boardroom table' story about a large manufacturing company that wanted to cut costs. One employee discovered that the organisation could save more than a billion dollars by using one supplier for their work gloves. To gain commitment and support from senior stakeholders, the employee gathered the 424 types of gloves, representing varying price points, to present on the boardroom table. This was an impactful way to communicate the folly and the money wasted, not only in the purchase itself, but also the transaction costs of managing numerous vendors.

Kotter's framework guides change plans and activity. It can be used to highlight the role of change leaders as well as change practitioners. It may appear as part of a change roadmap to demonstrate that the steps have been carefully considered in the change activity.

While Kotter's eight steps appear in many change plans, it's interesting to note that John Kotter himself refreshed his framework. In 2012 he published an article in *Harvard Business Review* titled 'Accelerate', in which he addresses a business environment of continuous and faster change that demands greater agility. He introduced the notion that such complexity in an organisation needs a dual operating system made up of *hierarchy* and *network.*

As a result, he repositioned his eight-step model as eight accelerators of change that represent the hierarchical element of the dual operating system. The network element in the dual system comprises **five principles**:

1. *Two systems, one organisation:*

    This approach acknowledges the role of the informal networks within an organisation.

2.   *Many change agents, including volunteers from across various roles:*

Instead of a few change agents who are usually in senior roles, broaden and diversify the scope and invite volunteers to join the group.

3.   *Shift to a 'want-to' and 'get-to' mindset from just a 'have-to' mindset:*

Inviting volunteers to be change agents promotes motivation, buy-in and co-creation.

4.   *Engage head AND heart, not just the head:*

Leverage passion and emotional involvement to drive the change.

5.   *A stronger focus on more leadership, instead of more management:*

Encourage acts of leadership to build a stronger network, inspiration and relationships.

Later, in 2014, *Accelerate* was published as a book by the same name and also spelled XLR8 on the book cover.

EMOTIONAL INTELLIGENCE (EI): DANIEL GOLEMAN

Often simply abbreviated to EI, the term *Emotional Intelligence* was first coined in the 1960s by Michael Beldoch and popularised in 1995 by American psychologist Daniel Goleman in his book titled *Emotional Intelligence*.

Emotional intelligence is the ability to be sufficiently self-aware to understand and regulate your own emotions, as well as make astute observations of the emotional state of others. According to Goleman, EI is made up of five elements:

1 | Self-Awareness

2 | Self-Regulation

3 | Motivation

4 | Empathy

5 | Social skills.

How it's applied

Whilst it's not explicitly or widely applied in change planning, EI is often cited as being a core capability of change leaders and change managers. In an organisation, it's most likely to appear in an organisational capability framework. The more capable you are in each of the five EI elements, the more effective you are likely to be as a change influencer.

⚲ GOOD TO KNOW

Emotional Intelligence (EI) is often referred to as Emotional Quotient (EQ).

PARTING WORDS

It's useful to be familiar with the key concepts in your field, as they provide a foundational understanding. You will hear or see them referenced in change plans or other change literature. While this list and overview is not exhaustive, it's a start to understanding some of the earlier thinking in this field. As you become more familiar with the foundational models, or seminal work, you will notice a great deal of alignment with change plans and approaches.

In an organisational context, many of these frameworks can help us understand human responses over time to an imposed change, particularly when people perceive that there is a great deal to lose when moving from the current state.

Whilst frameworks developed by pioneers such as Kurt Lewin continue to underpin the practice of change management, the interventions we implement need to be refined and tailored to address the unique challenges and requirements presented by the organisation at that point in time.

💡 GOOD TO KNOW

Showing alignment to change frameworks: Many large organisations develop their own change methodology. When this happens, it's common to see a diagram that shows alignment of in-house practice to existing, well-respected change frameworks to validate their approach.

OUR CHANGE FRAMEWORK
HOW IT ALIGNS TO BEST PRACTICE MODELS & FRAMEWORKS

OUR FRAMEWORK	INITIATE	PLAN	GET READY	EMBED
	Discover	Define & refine	Roll out changes	Empower

Kotter's 8 Steps	Sense of urgency	Guiding coalition	Communicate vision	Short term wins	
		Shared vision	Empower action	Consolidate gains	Embed new approaches

Prosci 3 Steps	PREPARING	MANAGING THE CHANGE	REINFORCING

Lewin 3 Phases	UNFREEZE	CHANGE	REFREEZE

You have to know the past

To understand the present

Carl Sagan

RELATED CHAPTERS: Change planning, Stakeholder engagement, Change measures, Change readiness, Change resistance

#

Whilst frameworks developed by pioneers such as Kurt Lewin continue to underpin the practice of change management, the interventions we implement need to be refined and tailored to address the unique challenges and requirements presented by the organisation at that point in time. #changeessentials.

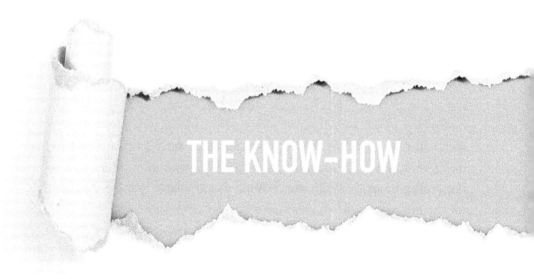

THE KNOW-HOW

9

CHANGE CAPABILITIES

You will hear recruiters and change managers refer to *change manage-ment capabilities*. If you work in a larger organisation which has an Enterprise Change Management Office, you are likely to see a statement of the change management capabilities, or a *capability framework*, that defines the expected skills required of the change practitioners as individuals.

We know from the chapter on *Enterprise Change Management*, that 'change' is also expressed as an organisational capability. For a business, this means: the overall ability to respond quickly to change; a commitment to build capability of senior leaders to guide others through ongoing change; and a commitment to clearly demonstrate the value of change manage-ment as an embedded practice in a centralised centre of excellence.

CAPABILITY FRAMEWORKS

Capability frameworks, sometimes called *competency frameworks*, provide clarity around the behaviours and skills demonstrated at different levels throughout the organisation. A **competency** is a set of skills, knowl-edge, abilities, attributes, experience, personality traits and motivators. Capability frameworks benefit both the organisation and the employee.

From an **organisational perspective**, these frameworks provide a clear definition of the competencies necessary for success and help to:

- Ensure that employees demonstrate sufficient expertise for their role
- Recruit and select new staff
- Evaluate performance
- Identify skill and competency gaps
- Provide more customised, focused training and professional development
- Enable employees and leaders with a common language around skills and development
- Plan for succession.

From an **employee's perspective**, a well understood competency framework enables them to:

- Understand the competencies currently relevant to their role
- Identify skill gaps, to address ways to do their jobs more effectively
- Prioritise professional development activity now and into the future
- Understand the pathways to progression within the organisation.

CHANGE CAPABILITIES

As mentioned in an earlier chapter, the role of the change practitioner is to advise, influence or be consulted on introducing and embedding the change. Their role is to ensure that the impacted people are ready to adopt the new ways. There is a set of functional and behavioural capabilities that forms part of their toolkit to do this.

A change practitioner should aim to have a broad set of capabilities made up of three parts:

1 | Core functional capabilities that specifically relate to their dedicated role

2 | Behavioural and general (non-change-specific) capabilities that complement their role, and are expected of change leaders and program/project directors

3 | Emerging capabilities.

CHANGE CAPABILITIES
THREE TYPES

CORE & FUNCTIONAL	BEHAVIOURAL	EMERGING
These are the **technical capabilities** that specifically relate to the change practitioner role.	These are more **generic capabilities** that are non-change specific and expected to be demonstrated in the change practitioner role.	These are the **newer capabilities** that prepare you for emerging business trends and help future-proof your career.

Each capability type provides the change practitioner with a different form of *skill fitness*, outlined in the table below. The core functional capabilities enable you to plan and support change delivery, typically in a more conventional end-to-end waterfall project. These are the skills we need for *match fitness* for our day-to-day activity. The more generic, behavioural capabilities are needed for *business fitness* and they serve us well in any role in an organisation. We must always consider our *evolutionary fitness* by looking out for emerging trends and the capabilities we need in a disruptive environment, and to future-proof our career.

CHANGE MASTERY

For change mastery, we need to be proficient in each of these three capability types:

CHANGE CAPABILITIES

CORE & FUNCTIONAL	BEHAVIOURAL	EMERGING
Change impact assessments	Emotional intelligence	Modern ways of working
Change planning & delivery	Strategic thinking	Human centred design
Stakeholder engagement	Empathy	Agile practices
Communications	Curiosity – in relentless quantities!	Digital literacy
Learning & performance support	Analysis & problem solving	Social media proficiency
Change readiness assessment	Networking & connecting	Hardwired human behaviour
Organisation design	Business acumen	
Project management principles		

If your employer doesn't have a change capability framework, or you don't have access to one, don't despair. Here's how the core change capabilities look with a short description.

CORE CHANGE CAPABILITY DEFINITIONS

Change impact assessments

A change consultant analyses activity in both the current and future states to identify the gap, and plan the change interventions to prepare people for the change. Looking beyond software development, the change practitioner needs to also assess the impacts to the people, processes, technology and external customers resulting from the change initiative.

Change planning and delivery

This is the ability to devise a plan that shows the approach, intent, resources and schedule of activities that will support successful delivery of the change initiative. Depending on the scope and scale of the project, this may be one or two pages, or a more detailed document. The change plan shows alignment to the business case or need for the change.

Business engagement and stakeholder management

Engagement with stakeholders involves creating information, forums and events to build support, acceptance and ultimately ownership of the change. The change manager plays a key role in helping the project team and sponsor to identify the key stakeholders, capture their details, plan activities such as workshops (which may differ for various stakeholder groups), and monitor their level of buy-in.

Communications

Large-scale change projects may employ dedicated communications specialists. In most cases, the change manager is responsible for the communications. This involves planning, developing and executing the communication to various stakeholder groups through a number of channels within the organisation. It may include monitoring and evaluating the effectiveness of the change communication.

Learning and performance support

This is the process of identifying the inputs required to plan for learning activity, and the outputs needed to support employee performance. For example, inputs such as data from change impact assessments are needed for learning needs analysis, to inform training plans and schedules. Outputs are learning events and user documentation such as Quick Reference Guides. It's about assessing, designing and implementing learning solutions to prepare people for the future state.

Change readiness

Change readiness activities ensure that the business and the impacted users are prepared for the change. In most change initiatives, this involves preparing business readiness checklists; for individuals there may be user readiness activities and checklists, along with change readiness surveys to monitor sentiment, awareness of and commitment to the change.

Organisation design

When a great deal of organisational re-design is taking place, specialists in this area will be called in. An understanding is helpful for change managers when initiatives involve changes to roles, Target Operating Models (TOMs) and organisational structures. Often this type of work is carried out alongside human resource specialists, as it may involve workforce transitions.

Project management principles

As most initiatives are run as projects, it's useful to know how to apply project management practices to change planning and delivery. This includes an understanding of project planning, project life cycles, governance, reporting, and risk management. For example, you will need to report change-management-related risks in the project risk register. Project governance requires reporting that needs input from change managers to report on change activity and milestones.

BEHAVIOURAL CAPABILITIES

The behavioural capabilities equip you with business fitness, and are not exclusive to change management. By looking at advertised positions for change professionals, you can see what is highly regarded. When you see descriptors such as 'outstanding communicator' and 'able to build effective working relationships with stakeholders' you can see a link to the core capabilities of communication and stakeholder engagement. Whilst the definitions of the core capabilities focus more on the technical aspects of the role, it's important to keep in mind the personal qualities that are also expected in an effective change practitioner.

Here are some personal qualities and behaviours that consistently appear in job adverts:

- Engaging
- Pragmatic
- Hands on
- Team player
- Comfortable with ambiguity and uncertainty
- Adaptive
- Collaborative
- Attention to detail
- Active listening skills.

EMERGING CAPABILITIES

The emerging capabilities are covered in greater detail in the last section of this book, titled *A brave new world*.

LEARNING ON THE JOB

Sometimes we miss learning opportunities that are right in front of us! Most of your learning will take place on the job by doing, through observation, and engagement with social networks.

If you are looking to get into change management, or are relatively new to the role, look for opportunities to build your skills and experience in these areas on the job, particularly in the core capabilities. If you are in an organisation with more experienced change professionals, ask if you can shadow them in some of their activities - for example, observing and helping at stakeholder engagement forums and impact assessment workshops. To learn different approaches, look for examples of change management plans, communication artefacts and other documents produced by peers.

Watch out for information sessions taking place in your organisation, such as *brown bag* or *lunch and learn* events. Not only will you learn from colleagues willing to share their expertise, but you will meet people from other parts of the business. Many organisations, or industry member-ships, provide access to subscriptions to industry research and eLearning modules, such as LinkedIn Learning. The Change Management Institute (CMI) runs short professional development sessions, some of which are open to non-members.

This is a good time to let you know of the numerous free resources you can find on my website, along with the generous sharing of expertise from other change professionals such as Dr Jen Frahm, in the form of blogs, podcasts, infographics, and short clips.

💡 GOOD TO KNOW

Take advantage of free networking events or meet-ups run by industry bodies in your area. Join social networking conversations inside and outside your organi-sation. Search 'meetup' on your browser, and you will be surprised at how many special interest groups exist and catch up!

In the next sections, titled *The know-how* and *This goes with that*, we take a closer look at the core capabilities:
- Change planning
- Change communication
- Stakeholder engagement
- Change impact assessments
- Learning and performance support
- Change readiness.

And in the last two sections, *Agile change management* and *A brave new world*, we cover the emerging capabilities:
- Agile change delivery and activity
- How change is changing
- Human-centred design: Where change management meets design thinking
- Communicating through different channels to co-create
- Brain-friendly change.

These are the emerging capabilities that will keep you relevant and demonstrate to recruiters and potential employers that you are committed to staying ahead of the curve.

RELATED CHAPTERS: All of them!

#

Take advantage of free networking events or meetups run by industry bodies in your area. Join social networking conversations inside and outside your organisation. #changeessentials.

10

CHANGE IMPACT ASSESSMENTS

When working on change implementation projects, and in conversations with people about the value of change management, I often hear the comment: 'Oh, change management, that's just communications and training, right?' Errr... no, not exactly! This is when the alarm bell goes off - the one that tells me it's time, yet again, to explode at least one commonly held myth about what change practitioners do.

We know from the list of core capabilities that there is so much more to change management than communications and training. On top of that, there's facilitation, coaching, the emerging capabilities, and understanding behavioural science for interventions. And of course, there's the assessment of change impacts.

While completing a change impact assessment is a core capability of a change practitioner, there is rarely any formal training or guidance provided on how to do this. Regardless of your project type - agile or waterfall, technology implementation, culture change, customer transformation or organisational restructure - an impact assessment is something a change consultant needs to complete as part of their role.

The capability is defined as: *assessing the impacts that will result from the planned change implementation in the areas of people, process, technology and customers.*

WHAT IS A CHANGE IMPACT ASSESSMENT?

In 1996, Robert Arnold and Shawn Bohner published a succinct and brilliant definition of a change impact analysis: *identifying the potential consequences of a change or estimating what needs to be modified to accomplish a change.* While this definition was crafted for software change impacts, it makes sense for all types of change.

On smaller projects, you may only need to complete a high-level impact assessment. For larger or more complex change initiatives, you may need to uncover more information with a more detailed impact assessment. The ability to understand the approach - including how to measure the level of impacts, how to complete and present the assessment, and how to use it as content for discussions with your impacted users and stakeholders - is an essential component of your change toolkit!

Either way, the change impact assessment helps you begin all your change planning with the end in mind.

WHY IT'S IMPORTANT

If you are ever asked why a change impact assessment is needed for your change initiative to succeed, here are five good reasons:

1. *It helps plan relevant CHANGE INTERVENTIONS:*

   In knowing the nature of the impacts and where they will occur, you have insights to plan your change approach, eg training, change champion networks, engagement forums, communications, super users, etc. This forms the backbone of your change plan.

2. *It drives DISCUSSION WITH STAKEHOLDERS:*

   Through visibility of impacts, it opens discussion with a common understanding of the scale of the change, who else is impacted, along with a common understanding of issues, challenges, resource allocation and other interventions needed.

3. *It determines overall SCOPE and SCALE of the change:*

    With a view of the scope and scale of the change, you can identify and mitigate any potential risks and issues before they arise. The *scale* is often represented as a rating to show no or little impact, to a high or significant impact. The *scope* is typically represented by change categories or dimensions, which can vary depending on the type of business. Many organisations, as a starting point, assess the categories of people, technology, process and customer impacts.

4. *It identifies hot spots for CHANGE EFFORT and collective IMPACTS across the business:*

    It provides a view of which business units and/or process groups and teams will be impacted the most and least; and it can be collated in one repository, so the impacts are represented as a heat map to show a single enterprise view.

5. *It shows the hot spots for OTHER CHANGE PROJECTS:*

    When liaising with other project teams, you can see a view of which business units and/or teams are impacted by other change projects. This will help with resource planning, ability to release SMEs and an indication of the capacity to absorb the change.

GETTING STARTED

There are three phases of change impact assessment:

1 | Early change assessment

2 | High-level impact assessment

3 | Detailed impact assessment.

PHASE ONE: *Early change assessment*

The *early change assessment* is one of the first things you carry out when you commence your change initiative, and the earlier the better. It can be completed in consultation with your project manager, who will be familiar with the business case.

The objective is to uncover early indicators of the scope and scale of the change, through asking a set of change assessment questions. Develop a set of questions to suit your business type by drawing on the business case and discussions with project team members. If your employer has an Enterprise Change Office, a set of standard questions may already be available. For each question, assign a rating of high, medium, low or no impact. Whilst it is usually too early to accurately assign a rating, it will provide the basis for further discussions.

QUESTIONS TO ASK

Here are a few early change assessment questions that apply to most business types:

- How many business units or organisational units will be affected?
- How dispersed are the impacted units? Are they located across geographies, within your own country, outside your country, in multiple locations, internationally?
- Does the change involve the introduction of new technology?
- Will people need to interact with technology and/or systems differently? Or use new technology/systems?
- How will people's roles change? Are there changes to existing roles, and/or newly created roles, and/or roles made redundant?
- How will processes change? Are there existing documented processes?
- Are there any current policies or legislation that will be affected, and/or need updating?
- Will people need to think and behave differently for this change to be successful, adopted or effective?
- How will external customers be affected by this change?

The answers to these questions will provide sufficient information for you to prepare a summary of likely impacts, and whether the impact in each area is likely to be high, medium or low. This will help you start planning the change activity.

PHASE TWO: High-level impact assessment

Using the information from the early change assessment, you can start to build a high-level impact assessment. Include this analysis in your change plan. There are many ways you can represent this. Here are some ideas. This table shows an example that includes a brief commentary on the gap analysis:

Impact Category	Current State	Future State	Gap	Impact Description	Impacted Group	Impact Rating
People	Describe the 'as is' state	Describe the 'to be' state	Describe the gap	Briefly describe the impact	Business units or teams	High Medium or Low?
Process						
Technology						
Customer						

This table shows an example of the high-level impacts by business unit:

Business Unit	No. of people	IMPACT CATEGORY			
		People	Process	Technology	Customer
Governance and Legal	20	MEDIUM	HIGH	HIGH	LOW
Operations	35	LOW	LOW	MEDIUM	N/A
Finance	15	MEDIUM	MEDIUM	MEDIUM	MEDIUM
Technology	35	MEDIUM	MEDIUM	MEDIUM	LOW
Sales and Marketing	40	HIGH	HIGH	HIGH	HIGH
Human Resources	15	MEDIUM	HIGH	LOW	N/A
TOTAL	**160**				

In your change plan, it's a good idea to represent high, medium and low with colours. Use red for high impact, yellow or orange for medium impact, green for low impact and white for no impact.

GOOD TO KNOW

The high-level impact assessment can be represented on a poster size sheet of paper with coloured post-it notes designating high, medium and low, on your visual management board. This will generate interest from people passing by and promote ad hoc conversations that may not have otherwise occurred. For example, a stakeholder or impacted user from Operations may walk past and see that their impact is rated as low, yet they may uncover additional insights that suggest the impact to their business area is high.

CHANGE IMPACT CATEGORIES

A *change impact category* is the term used to describe the nature of the impact. Common to most organisational change projects are the four categories of *people, process, technology* and *customer*. Assign a description to each impact category that is relevant for your organisation. Here's an example:

CHANGE IMPACT ASSSESSMENTS
IMPACT CATEGORIES AND DESCRIPTIONS

people	process	technology	customer
Changes to organisational structure, roles or responsibilities, skills and knowledge, workload, capability requirements, performance measures. For culture change, the extent to which new/different behaviours and mindsets are required.	Changes to the way things are done, the processes, systems used, e.g. the capture/use of new business data, interactions with other business areas etc.	Changes to systems that are used, how technology operates, interfaces to upstream/downstream systems, look and feel of screens, user access and interface, reporting capability.	Changes that will have an impact on our customers or the way our customers interact with our business.

IMPACT CATEGORY BY SCALE

Once you have identified and defined impact categories relevant to your organisation, further define them as high, medium and low impacts. This will provide a transparent description to your stakeholders and end users on how the impacts are rated, as well as a useful framework for further impact conversations and assessments.

Impact Category	Impact Description	Impact Level Ratings			
		High	Medium	Low	N/A
Technology	Scope of changes to technology and tools	Technology, data and transactions are completely new or current technology is significantly changed.	Some change to existing technology/ tools/ functionality, data and/ or transactions.	Minor change to existing technology/ tools/ functionality, data and/or transactions.	No changes or impact to technology and tools.
	Example	Total system replacement or significant Impacts to multiple downstream systems identified.	Impacts to a number of downstream systems identified.	Some impacts to downstream systems identified.	N/A

PHASE THREE: Detailed impact assessment

The *detailed impact assessment* expands on the high-level analysis with additional detail on the current and future states, such as details on end-to-end processes. This level of analysis is often captured on a spreadsheet. For smaller initiatives or an agile project, it may not be required.

The insights you discover in the high-level impact gap analysis and any further detailed change impact assessments will be helpful input into the training needs analysis and learning content development.

There are many ways to source the information needed for detailed impact assessments:

- Business stakeholders and Subject Matter Experts (SMEs)
- Workshops
- Journey maps - current state and future state
- Business requirements documentation
- Process documentation
- One-on-one meetings
- Position descriptions
- Shadowing impacted end users.

HANDY TIPS FOR ALL PHASES OF THE CHANGE IMPACT ASSESSMENT:

- Use the insights to drive conversations with your stakeholders and end users
- Be intensely curious... ask questions
- You can apply this change impact approach to all types of change
- The process is iterative - you will uncover new information as you go, so impact assessments are regularly refreshed
- Apply document control to your iterations so you have a history of changes and who requested them.

💡 GOOD TO KNOW

You may see change impact levels depicted as *Harvey Balls*. Before I landed in change management, I had seen my fair share of Harvey Balls but had no idea what they were called; so imagine my confusion when my Change Lead said to me, 'Oh, just use Harvey Balls to show the impact levels'.

A Harvey Ball is a round icon that is shaded differently to visually represent a measure or outcome, and can be created in PowerPoint or downloaded as an icon. For example, if you want to represent five levels of impact, your Harvey Balls would look like this:

CHANGE IMPACT ASSSESSMENTS
HARVEY BALLS

EXAMPLE FOR FIVE LEVELS OF IMPACT

VERY HIGH $- ->$ LOW / NONE

RELATED CHAPTERS: Change planning, Learning and performance support

The change impact assessment is a great tool to kick off conversations with stakeholders and to get on the same page with a common understanding. #changeessentials.

CHANGE PLANNING

In my early days in change management, the change plan was almost always a multi-page Word document, with several reviewers and approvers who needed to sign it off. For very large programs of work, this is still likely to be the same. Quite often, this document was approved and then filed away, hardly ever seen again. Since then, change plans have become more succinct and visual, mostly represented as a PowerPoint deck of slides.

Every change consultant needs to know how to complete a change plan, and this capability is defined as: *the ability to analyse, scope and develop a plan that is aligned with the business case, with recommended activities and interventions that will successfully execute the change initiatives.*

The change plan is completed in the early phase of the project, after you carry out your early change impact assessment. Your plan shows what is changing, and the relevant activity that will be carried out by change team members for a specific initiative. The process of completing the change plan is valuable because it:

- acts as a source document for engagement with the project team and stakeholders
- showcases how the key change activities support the project and business objectives
- guides the change practitioner through the planning approach.

GOOD TO KNOW

As organisations are becoming more agile, change management documentation is becoming lighter and more visual. In more recent times, I've noticed that many change plans start as a *plan on a page* or *change canvas*, and a more detailed change plan (where required) builds on this information.

Most of the elements that make up the change plan have a dedicated chapter in this book.

WHAT TO INCLUDE IN THE CHANGE PLAN

The change plan typically includes the following content:

Theme	Typical content
Statement of alignment	Business and project objectives.
	Change management activity will support benefits realisation by addressing the people side of the change.
	Handy Tip: Use the business case to source this information.
What's changing?	The key changes that this project will deliver.
	This can be described as: now we do this; in the future state we will do that; eg *as is* (current state), and contrast to the *to be* (future state).
	See chapter: Change impact assessments.
Change management approach	The change approach or methodology in place at the organisation, and how this plan aligns to that.
	See example later in this chapter.
Key stakeholders and stakeholder analysis	A table showing each name, title, project role, and which project team member will manage the relationship with each key stakeholder.
	A statement or diagram showing how stakeholders will be assessed to determine their level of engagement.

Theme	Typical content
	A stakeholder engagement plan with the key activities that will keep them informed and engaged throughout the lifecycle of the project. *See chapter: Stakeholder engagement.*
Communications	The communications schedule, which outlines key messages that will be distributed to key stakeholders and end users throughout the lifecycle of the project. A table with the high-level communication plan that shows the audience, the communication channel/s, the key messages, frequency or key dates for communication, who writes it, who approves and who sends. *See chapters: Change communication, Change champions.*
Impacted users	A table showing which business units or user groups are impacted, why they are impacted, approximately how many people there are, their location/s and if the impact is likely to be high, medium or low. For visual impact, colour code this in red, amber or green. *See chapter: Change impact assessments.*
Customer experience	If the external customer is impacted, explain how the customer experience (CX) will change, and the opportunities this presents.
Learning and development approach	The learning approach outlines high-level learning needs and audience groups, and defines the level of impact to these people. Refer to further information that may be captured in a separate document, eg Learning Needs Analysis, training schedules, more detailed learning plan. *See chapter: Learning and performance support.*

Theme	Typical content
Assessing change readiness	How change readiness will be assessed and what will be done with the results.
	Refer to further information that may be captured in a separate document.
	See chapter: Change readiness.
Change risks and issues	Identify change-related risks and issues, and how these will be mitigated.
	See Chapter: Project management and change management.
High-level roadmap	Visual roadmap of key change activity across the life cycle of the project.
	See chapters: Change communications, Communicate to co-create.
Change goals and adoption/success measures	List the specific change management goals for the project, and how the success of these goals will be measured.
	See chapters: Change measures, Making change stick.
Costing estimates	List expected costs associated with carrying out the proposed change management activities. Present the costs in a table.
	See chapter: Change costs.
Key roles and responsibilities	Explain roles of change team members, project team members, change champions and super users, to clarify key responsibilities.
	See chapter: Roles in change management.
Document version control	It's robust project practice to include version control on most of your change artefacts, especially ones that are continually updated and the ones that require review and approval for sign-off.
	Exceptions to this are highly visual documents, which are often drawn from pages from the *change plan*, such as the *change canvas* and the *change roadmap*.

The *change plan* prompts the change consultant to probe and investigate the people side of the change, as well as providing an indication of the *scope* and *scale* of the change. The *scope* of the change tells us how widely across the organisation the impact will be experienced. The *scale* of the change is about the degree of impact. A change initiative may have broad *scope* by affecting all employees in the business, but it may be a small change in *scale* that requires little or no effort in terms of training, communication and adoption.

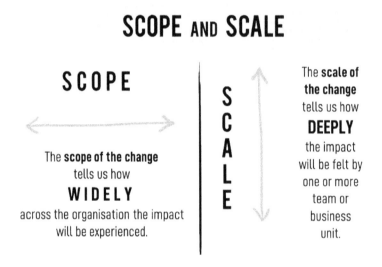

SCOPE AND SCALE

SCOPE

The **scope of the change** tells us how **WIDELY** across the organisation the impact will be experienced.

SCALE

The **scale of the change** tells us how **DEEPLY** the impact will be felt by one or more team or business unit.

CHANGE PLAN ON A PAGE

For simplicity and ease of reading, the *change plan on a page*, or the *change canvas*, is a brilliant one-page view of the change management intent and activity. It usually includes the case for the change and provides early insights into the scope of the initiative, helping build rationale for dedicated change management resources.

If your project has a visual management board where key information is posted, add a poster size version of your change canvas so it's highly visible. When it's on a wall, you can add or amend information in discussions with your project team members and your relevant stakeholders.

Leave open space on your canvas, and invite comments and questions on post-it notes.

The change canvas is one of the documents I carry around with me (in A3 size) to drive and support my change conversations. Here's an example of one I've used that can be easily adapted to your initiative:

THE CHANGE CANVAS
AN EXAMPLE

PRODUCT OWNER..	CHANGE LEAD...................................
Change being introduced.............................	Date...

Problem (the WHAT)	Solution (the HOW)	Value Proposition (the WHY)

Customers/stakeholders (WHO)		Time & effort needed/change resources

- COMMUNICATION -

Existing channels	Key messages – W I I F M

Success criteria	Risks & issues (high level)

© Lena Ross 2016

CHANGE APPROACH

A step-by-step change approach shows stakeholders the planned sequence of change activity and acts as a guideline for the change management team.

In large organisations with an Enterprise Change Management Office, there is likely to be an established change methodology or framework. This change approach is likely to be aligned to the organisation's preferred project methodology. Include it in your change plans to show the series of planned events.

Even when working on agile projects, a view of your approach will be useful.

In this example, the organisation's change approach also shows the alignment with Kurt Lewin's three phases and John Kotter's eight-step model:

CHANGE ROADMAP

Another one-pager I develop for all change initiatives, that remains available and visible in a poster or A3 format, is the *calendar of key change activity*. You may also add key project milestones to show how the change management activity is scheduled to support project delivery.

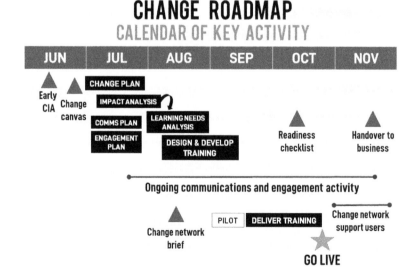

The one-page change canvas and your change roadmap are ideal documents to display and carry with you for discussions, particularly with senior stakeholders and your sponsor, who usually has a preference for a high-level view.

Many of the following chapters further explain the core change capabilities along with the activities and artefacts that the change consultant delivers to execute the change plan.

RELATED CHAPTERS: Change impact assessments, Stakeholder engagement, Change communications, Learning and performance support, Change costs, Change measures, Making change stick

As organisations are becoming more agile, change management documentation is becoming lighter and more visual. In more recent times, I've noticed that many change plans start as a *plan on a page* or *change canvas*, and a more detailed change plan (where required) builds on this information. #changeessentials.

The change plan prompts the change consultant to probe and investigate the people side of the change, as well as providing an indication of the *scope* and *scale* of the change. #changeessentials.

**CHANGE
COMMUNICATIONS**

Change communication ensures that those impacted by the change understand why the change is necessary, and what they need to do differently to support and embed the change. As a change management capability, communications is defined as: *being able to develop communication and implement communication activities that support the many stakeholder groups impacted by the change.*

The change communication plan is a key change management artefact because it identifies and provides detail for the change initiative on:

- What are the key messages
- The purpose of specific messages
- Who are the audience groups
- The communications channels that will be leveraged
- When the communications will be sent, and frequency if regular updates are required
- Who sends which messages
- Who may need to approve the messages.

This information can be captured in a summary table:

Purpose	Key Message/s	Audience	Channel	When	From Whom

PURPOSE

The overall purpose of communication is to inform and engage. This may sound relatively simple, but it's helpful to be clear on why the communication is taking place. Your communication may be just to inform, or you may want the reader to take action. For example, you may request that impacted users activate a new account and set up a password, or test a new feature on their devices; or it may be a request to complete a short survey or readiness assessment questionnaire.

Other communication could include guidance or learning material such as Frequently Asked Questions (FAQs), Quick Reference Guides (QRGs) or requests to select and book into training sessions.

IDENTIFYING KEY MESSAGES

When identifying the key points to be communicated, it's a good idea to consult senior stakeholders who represent each business unit. Ask them:

- What the key messages should be to help you write the communication
- Their preferred channels
- If there are any stories they can share with their teams to personalise the message.

Key messages may include:

- Business benefits - why we need to change
- What will change
- What remains the same
- Milestones and timelines of key activity
- Engagement forums - how people can get involved and have their say; any change readiness surveys that may be taking place; Q & A sessions; project showcases
- Performance support that will be available after implementation

- Benefits for the individual and for each team or stakeholder group - this is called the WIIFM, an abbreviation for 'what's in it for me'
- What will happen if we don't embrace the change - the risks of not changing.

AUDIENCE GROUPS

There will be various stakeholder groups and impacted user groups to consider. Include your project control group and steering committees in your stakeholder audiences. This will help you develop your key messages for each group.

- Use your stakeholder map or matrix to check that all key audience groups/stakeholders are included in your *communication and engagement plan*
- Identify which messages need to be tailored for specific stakeholder groups
- Include your change champions as a stakeholder group and think about how they can *cascade* key messages
- Don't forget your Project Steering Committee.

Planning for audience groups

On larger projects, where you are developing different messages for various user groups, a table for each group may be helpful:

Audience group	<insert group, team or business unit>
Communication	
Channel	
Sent from	
Key message	
Purpose/call to action	
Timing	
Who needs to review message	

Audience group	<insert group, team or business unit>
<insert body of message>	

CHANNELS

To ensure broad coverage of key messages and address individual preferences, tap into a range of communications channels including online, face-to-face and email.

- Look out for existing channels such as regular team meetings, where leaders can provide updates on the change initiative. For these, develop a list of FAQs or *talking points* to create a dedicated email inbox as a first point of communication from employees. Use it to send meeting and event invites. This channel is usually monitored by the project analyst or co-ordinator.
- Include less formal, two-way communication channels. An enterprise social network group for the program or project provides a forum for interaction and regular *ad hoc* program updates, photos, back-channelling from key events and activities, and links to relevant information.
- A popular communication channel is a regular project postcard. Short and visual, the postcard is emailed with a project-branded banner to key stakeholders. Store all issues on the project's SharePoint site or a similar central location, so it can easily be located and accessed by all. Create a post on your enterprise social network with a link to the postcard. The postcard features updates, milestones and what's coming up. Send it fortnightly or monthly.

- Self-Serve Options: A dedicated SharePoint site as a one-stop shop for employees to find out about the change initiative. It can feature photos, project postcards, links to enterprise social networks, how to contact key project people, a calendar of events, noticeboard and frequently asked questions (FAQs).
- Multi Media: As most people have portable devices, it's easy to take short *ad hoc* clips during activities and engagement events, visual showcase walls, site visits, and other interesting program information. The objective is to provide updates in a media clip format that's informal yet informative.

FREQUENCY AND RHYTHM

The communications calendar

The frequency and rhythm of change communications is often captured in a visual calendar. This is another artefact that can feature on your project visual management board.

COMMUNICATIONS CALENDAR

CHANNELS	JUL	AUG	SEP	OCT	NOV	DEC
Face to face	Lean Coffee	Town Hall	Lean Coffee	Showcase	Town Hall	Lean Coffee
Project Postcard	✉	✉	✉	✉	✉	✉
Intranet	Set up site					
Enterprise Social Network		Kick off group	Yam Jam		Yam Jam	
Visual Management	Set up wall	Introduce personas	Kanban			
Existing Forums	Steering Committee ◆ GM Bi-Monthly Meeting ◇	◆	◆ ◇	◆	◆ ◇	◆

THE COMMUNICATORS

Business rationale for the change

The change sponsor is the person to communicate the business reasons for the change initiative. The case for change often includes the business benefits, and positions the change initiative in the context of market forces and competitor activity. It's ideal if the sponsor communicates beyond a faceless email channel. When a sponsor makes themselves visible through social enterprise networks and face-to-face events such as town halls and project showcases, they also have the opportunity to engage in conversations to personalise the change and be perceived as both visible and approachable.

How the change affects different teams

More recent research continues to support findings from as early as the 1980s, about the person from whom employees prefer to hear most of the messages about the change.

The *Prosci Best Practices in Change Management Benchmarking Report 2018* indicates that the *preferred sender* of communications for *personal level messages* is the employee's direct manager. Personal level messages contrast with organisation-focused messages. This is consistent with findings from previous research carried out by Prosci, suggesting that this preference has remained constant for some time. Results show that the direct manager or team leader is clearly the preferred communicator of the change for *personal messages*, with 67% of the 1,778 participants responding with this preference. These findings suggest people trust that their immediate manager can explain how the change will impact their immediate teams.

ENTERPRISE VIEW

It's common to find a number of projects taking place in an organisation at the same time. You can take an enterprise view when planning your communication by engaging with change leads from the other projects. An understanding of what is taking place with other key engagement activity and milestones, particularly when impacting the same end users and stakeholder groups, will help you consider the scheduling of milestones, key messages and events. Applying an enterprise lens to communications may uncover synergies in key messages or flag specific periods when your own project's messages may be diluted or lost.

EXTERNAL CUSTOMERS

Where external customers are impacted, reach out to the dedicated communications team in your organisation. The external communications team has the expertise in developing messages and collateral for external business partners, including customers. They are familiar with organisational protocols, any legal ramifications, and the tone and language that is used to engage with specific customer groups.

EVALUATING THE EFFECTIVENESS OF CHANGE COMMUNICATION

How will you know that your communications and engagement plans are hitting the mark? Identify the way you plan to gather feedback on your communications and what success looks like. You can gain valuable insights on how your communication is tracking by:

- Questions
- Action taken - eg survey participation, logins
- Change readiness - awareness levels
- Enterprise social network - you can see social media metrics such as members in your group; look beyond how many people are just 'liking' the posts and check how many people are weighing in with comments or sharing your content

- Intranet - check site visits, unique visitors
- Observable changes in the behaviours, actions or language used by users
- Feedback from stakeholders and change champions.

A word on social media metrics

A great deal has been written about how to measure the success of your social media activity. When you check out the numerous articles on the internet, you're likely to come across the term *vanity metrics*. This term was coined by Eric Ries in a blog post in 2009 to describe measures that mean very little on their own, such as the number of followers, page views and subscribers. On their own, these measures may appear impressive, but for more meaningful data, we need to look beyond vanity metrics and explore ratios. Interestingly, Eric Ries went on to write his successful book *The Lean Startup* in 2011.

Instead of this...	Measure this for awareness	Measure this for engagement
Enterprise social network group members	Membership/follower *growth rate* compared to other groups. How quickly are you attracting group members? *#new members/#all members x 100*	Percentage of active users vs group members How many are liking, commenting and sharing? *#active users/#all members x 100*
Page views/visits	Percentage who click through vs page views. *#click throughs/#total page views x 100*	Number of downloads or action required, eg respond to invitation or request further information. *#action completed on page/#total page views x 100*
Email open rate	Percentage who click through to links *#click throughs/#total email recipients x 100*	Call to action is carried out, for example a link to a survey. *#action completed/#total email recipients x 100*

☝ GOOD TO KNOW

Assign a hashtag to your change initiative for your enterprise social network. Not only does the hashtag make it easy for you and others to search for relevant posts on your project, it also enhances online identity.

By monitoring and assessing the effectiveness of your change communications, you will be able to adjust course and fine-tune your communications approach as required.

These will form part of your change measures, covered in greater detail in a later chapter.

☝ GOOD TO KNOW

You can download the executive summary of the *Prosci Best Practices in Change Management Benchmarking Report 2018* from their website.

RELATED CHAPTERS: Change measures, Communicate to co-create

#

Change communication ensures those impacted by the change understand why the change is necessary, and what they need to do differently to support and embed the change. #changeessentials.

#

Assign a hashtag to your change initiative for your enterprise social network. Not only does the hashtag make it easy for you and others to search for relevant posts on your project, it also enhances online identity. #changeessentials.

By monitoring and assessing the effectiveness of your change communications, you will be able to adjust course and fine-tune your communications approach as required. #changeessentials.

13

STAKEHOLDER ENGAGEMENT

One of the core capabilities of the change practitioner is stakeholder management and engagement. This capability is defined as: *the ability to identify and engage stakeholder groups to build support, acceptance and ownership of the change.* At the less experienced end, the change role is to support the identification of stakeholders and create and maintain the stakeholder matrix.

The change practitioner's role is to develop, in consultation with the project leadership team and/or the senior sponsors, an engagement plan that considers:

- Buy-in and level of participation required from stakeholders
- Anticipated resistance and proposed interventions
- Optimal channels and/or forums for face-to-face engagement, with identification of stakeholder communication preferences
- Clear ownership of stakeholder relationships for consistent messages
- Strategies to build strong partnerships
- Potential conflicting interest with other organisational events or related programs and projects taking place
- The relationships between stakeholders - can one stakeholder influence another?

There is a general consensus that stakeholder engagement is important and often needs the expertise that the change professional brings to the program. The change plan provides details on stakeholders, and planned activity to build and maintain their engagement throughout the life cycle of the project. However, when carrying out a Post-Implementation Review (PIR) or retrospective, stakeholder relationships are often identified as one thing many project teams wish they had done better.

STAKEHOLDER TYPES

Your stakeholder group will be made up of decision makers and influencers.

Decision makers

The *decision makers* are critical stakeholders in a senior executive role who can *stop* or *significantly delay* the project. They determine and steer strategic direction and will ensure that the project's activity is aligned with the organisational strategy.

The influencers

The *influencers* may not have the positional authority to stop or delay the project, but they are often trusted advisors or recommenders to senior executives. As respected employees, they provide valuable input, are able to motivate others to take action, and will escalate issues.

💡 **GOOD TO KNOW**

Informal influence is just as effective as formal influence from senior stakeholders.

HOW INFORMAL INFLUENCE WORKS

Let's imagine we are in 1775 at the start of the American Revolution. Two revolutionaries, Paul Revere and William Dawes, set out on a horseback journey to spread the word to unite the country in the 'cause'. While Revere and Dawes cover the same distance and towns, with the same message, it is only Revere's message that garners the level of passion and support for the change. In his book, *The Tipping Point,* Malcolm Gladwell identified Revere's approach and social presence as the ingredient that 'tipped' the message, and describes people with Revere's 'rare set of social gifts' as connectors, mavens and salesmen.

Paul Revere wasn't in a role that held positional power, such as politician or community leader. Yet his informal influence altered the course of history. He was a silversmith who was well connected, and with social presence. He belonged to numerous clubs representing diverse interests. He knew who to reach out to, in order to spread the message.

This story reminds us that we need to look further than stakeholders in the organisation with formal, positional power. We also need to consider the hidden influencers. They may not have that formal power, but they do have social power and respect.

GETTING STARTED

High-level stakeholder map

A good way to build your list of stakeholders is to gather your project team and place all stakeholder names on a map with all business units represented. This visual representation, rather than a linear capture on a spreadsheet, will help your team members see possible connections, relationships or duplication.

You may also have stakeholders who are outside your organisation, such as vendors or business partners.

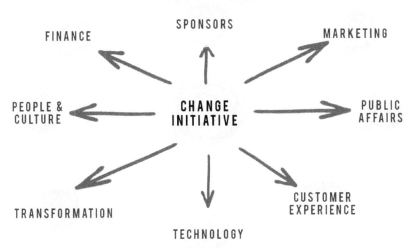

The stakeholder matrix

The stakeholder matrix, usually created in a spreadsheet, is a common way to record the names of the people you need to engage throughout the project. This matrix can capture additional detail such as impact levels, current levels of commitment, level of influence, preferred methods of communication, and primary stakeholder relationship owner.

Name	Business Unit	Level of Commitment	Current Level of Support	Influence	Preferred Communication Channel	Relationship Owner	Forums Events
		High, medium or low?					

Use this information to plan appropriate change activities.

This change artefact is refreshed regularly throughout the project life cycle, so it's a good idea to maintain document and version control so you can view previous versions when needed.

MATRIX ALTERNATIVES

There are several good models that take a mapping approach to stakeholders that's more visual than a conventional matrix spreadsheet approach.

The power/interest grid

The power/interest grid is a popular framework to group stakeholders and prioritise engagement activity and effort.

In this framework, power is usually interpreted as formal power, which is easy to identify by organisational hierarchy, as it's based on position and title.

The level of interest in the change may be difficult to measure at first. You may need to assess this with a change readiness assessment or short survey of your stakeholders. The best way to gauge interest is by asking people. Grouping stakeholders on a grid can be subjective and needs a discussion with the stakeholder relationship owners, who are usually members of your project team.

STAKEHOLDER ANALYSIS
POWER – INTEREST GRID

POWER ↕

HIGH

| KEEP SATISFIED | MANAGE CLOSELY |

LOW   INTEREST ↔   HIGH

| MONITOR | KEEP INFORMED |

LOW

With each stakeholder group, change consultants typically identify engagement actions as a guideline, as shown in this table:

Keep Satisfied *High Power, Low Interest*	**Manage Closely** *High Power, High Interest*
Latents.	Promoters, key players who can **stop** or **delay** your project.
Engage and consult to find an area of interest, hot button.	Focus efforts on this group.
Aim to increase level of interest.	Involve in governance, decision making.
Monitor *Low Power, Low Interest*	**Keep Informed** *Low Power, High Interest*
Apathetic.	Defenders who can be great **advocates** for your project.
Keep in the loop with general newsletters, intranet updates.	Show consideration, change champs, leverage the energy.
Aim to move to High Interest, especially if they start to make noise.	

Stakeholder commitment

You can assess the level of stakeholder commitment to your change initiative by applying Conner's and Patterson's commitment throughout the project lifecycle. This curve is often simplified (see diagram below) to assess stakeholders' readiness and acceptance of the change in four stages, so you can plan ahead, manage and mitigate potential or real resistance to the change. With the planned activities and change interventions, you can expect stakeholders to move from one position on the curve to the next.

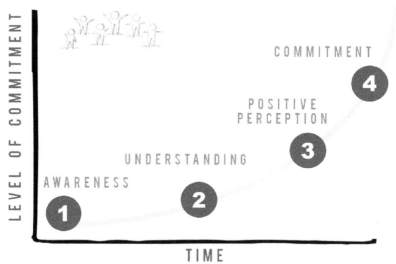

COMMITMENT CURVE

SOURCE: Based on Conner & Patterson Commitment Curve, *Training and Development Journal*, 1982, Vol.36, No.4

In discussions with your project team members, assess each stakeholder's level of commitment on the curve. Define what each level may look like, as shown in this example:

Awareness	Understanding	Positive Acceptance	Commitment
People realise the change is coming.	People not only realise the change is coming, but comprehend what the change is and *how* it will impact them and *why* it's happening.	People accept the new way of working and are positive about what the change will mean for themselves, the business and their customers.	People believe in the change and actively commit themselves to the new way of working.

DRIVING STAKEHOLDER DISCUSSIONS

We know that effective stakeholder planning and engagement goes beyond the stakeholder matrix. Change practitioners add a great deal of value by helping project leadership teams to facilitate regular discussions to:

- Identify stakeholder priorities
- Agree on key messages and communication channels
- Review movement on the change commitment curve
- Uncover additional hidden influencers in the organisation and areas of potential resistance and support.

This means that the stakeholder matrix, with its numerous updates, is simply an output of the rich and valuable discussions with your project team. In between these scheduled discussions, talk about your stakeholders more frequently in project team meetings. As a regular agenda item, the project team will keep stakeholder relationships top of mind.

💡 GOOD TO KNOW

Your stakeholder information is confidential data: A stakeholder matrix is a document that often contains sensitive information such as a stakeholder's level of commitment, potential challenges and how they may be addressed by the stakeholder owner. For this reason, make sure this artefact is stored in a place that does not have public access. For example, do *not* store it on your organisation's shared drive. On some projects, this artefact has also been password protected for access by the project team members only.

ᕯ GOOD TO KNOW

After running any meetings or workshops on stakeholder commitment, be sure to remove all flipchart sheets, post-it notes, and particularly any notes on a whiteboard - especially check whiteboards that have a rotating writing surface. On more than one occasion, I've found names on whiteboards in meeting rooms that should have been erased.

RELATED CHAPTERS: Change planning, Change readiness

In stakeholder management and engagement, look beyond people with formal, positional power. Look for the hidden influencers who may not have formal power, but do have social power and respect. #changeessentials.

Effective stakeholder planning and engagement goes beyond the stakeholder matrix. Change practitioners add a great deal of value by helping project leadership teams to facilitate regular discussions to discuss engagement. #changeessentials.

14

LEARNING AND
PERFORMANCE
SUPPORT

While dedicated training specialists are employed on many change initiatives, the responsibility of managing the end-to-end training of impacted users often lies with the change practitioner, making it a core change management capability. The process of analysing training needs, and designing and delivering learning, provides numerous opportunities to engage with impacted users and build change champion networks to co-create learning solutions. It's no surprise, therefore, that change management attracts many people with a background in learning and development.

For change practitioners, there is an expectation that as a core capability they can a*ssess, design, implement and evaluate learning solutions that support business change and impacted users' transition needs.* Training or learning as a change activity ensures that the people impacted by the change understand why the change is taking place, and what they need to do differently to support the change in the future state.

Each change initiative you work on will be different. However, understanding the principles of Learning and Development is helpful.

IN YOUR CHANGE PLAN

It's likely that you will reference learning and performance support as an activity in your change plan. To represent your high-level learning approach visually, you can include a table that shows:

- User group/audience
- Key content or learning outcomes
- Location of audience
- How many people are expected to need training
- The skill or capability gap the training will address
- How the training may be delivered.

Once you kick off the change activity, you'll uncover more details to develop your learning plan and approach. For example, the impact assessment will inform the gaps between the current state and future state, to help you identify the actual training need.

ON SMALL PROJECTS

For small projects, you can capture your training activity in a high-level plan that looks like this:

Describe the impact	High-level training need	Who is impacted?	Key content covered	Proposed training delivery method

At a glance, this table shows:

- A brief description of each impact
- How each impact translates to the training need, to show why the training is necessary
- Who is impacted and will need the training, so you have identified a stakeholder group
- The key training content, which uncovers what the impacted users will need to do differently to support and embed the change

- How the training will be delivered, eg face-to-face learning, via eLearning modules, Quick Reference Guides.

TRANSLATING THE IMPACTS TO LEARNING NEEDS

The first phase in learning design is the learning or training needs analysis, often abbreviated to LNA or TNA.

On a change initiative, a great deal of the content that informs the learning needs analysis is the impact assessment. We know from the previous chapter that by completing a change impact assessment, we discover what people will need to do differently in the way they follow a process, or interact with their place of work and technology, as well as their customers and other team members.

 GOOD TO KNOW

The impact assessment helps you *begin with the end in mind*. With a view of what is affected in the areas of skills, behaviours, processes and technology required to support the future state, you are able to plan training with that end view in mind.

This is a little different to how conventional training needs analyses are carried out, where current levels of capability are assessed to establish a benchmark. In a change initiative, the current state is the benchmark. Instead of the defined gap being specific to a competency or skill, the focus is on the gap between the *current state* and the *future state*.

Despite this difference in the purpose of identifying the learning needs, the approach taken to develop a learning program still follows best practice learning design.

LEARNING DESIGN CYCLE

Best practice learning design follows a four-phase cycle:

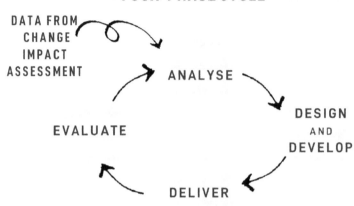

LEARNING & DEVELOPMENT
FOUR PHASE CYCLE

DATA FROM
CHANGE
IMPACT
ASSESSMENT

ANALYSE

DESIGN
AND
DEVELOP

EVALUATE

DELIVER

Assess & Analyse	Design & Develop	Deliver	Evaluate
Look at impact assessments. Work with stakeholders from each user group to uncover preferred training channels. What support is required to validate content that needs to be covered to build the capability needed in the future state?	Plan logistics/ schedule. Write session outlines. Prepare learning documentation for participants, eg slide decks, handouts, online resources, quick reference guides/job aids. Assess if vendor input is needed.	Manage the implementation of training, either face-to-face and/ or through digital channels. Plan for knowledge transfer to business after implementation. Plan logistics - where it will take place?	Evaluate the effectiveness of the training activity through feedback surveys and adoption measures.

Assess & Analyse	Design & Develop	Deliver	Evaluate
Outputs			
· Learning Needs Analysis	· Schedule · Budget	· Attendance records · Training material · Performance support plan and reference material	· Completed evaluations · Report on summary of evaluations · Adoption measures

LEARNING PLAN

A larger project or program of work will usually need a more detailed *learning plan*. This document typically explains all the phases in the learning cycle, and includes a roadmap that shows key activity and artefacts for the end users.

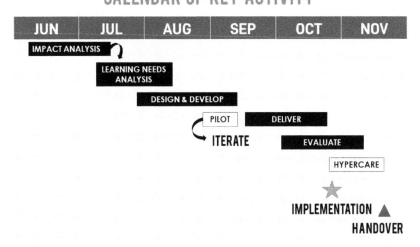

Contents of the learning plan may include information on:

- *Learning Needs Analysis:* What it is, how it will be carried out with inputs required, why it's important, how many people will need training.
- *Design and development:* Learning curriculum, high-level timeline of key activity.
- *Development:* Learning materials that will be produced, SME input required, defining and agreeing on learning outcomes, review and approval of content.
- *Delivery:* Learning schedules and delivery methods such as face-to-face and/or eLearning, locations, any pilot programs, who will deliver the training, post training user support or support documentation, eg Frequently Asked Questions, Quick Reference Guides.
- *Evaluation:* How feedback from participants will be gathered and reported.
- *A statement of what is in scope and what is out of scope:* For example, out of scope may be 'ongoing training in the Business as Usual environment post-implementation'.
- *Cost estimate:* How much will it cost to design, develop and deliver the training?
- *Hypercare:* A period of performance support immediately following implementation.
- *Handover of documentation to the business:* This includes agreement with the business about responsibility and ownership.

Some typical documents a change practitioner will prepare are:

- Learning needs analysis
- Learning and performance support plan or approach
- Post-implementation support plan
- Learning schedule
- Learning material
- Learning evaluation forms

- Learning evaluation reports
- Learning material to hand over to Business as Usual.

Depending on the scope and scale of your change initiative, learning plans may require engagement with: external vendors (training providers or vendor providing the systems); subject matter experts from different parts of the business; dedicated learning professionals and instructional designers working on your project; and your change champions.

WHO DELIVERS THE TRAINING?

Once you determine the type of training and the actual content that is needed to prepare your impacted users for the future state, you will have an idea of the expertise needed to design and deliver the learning. This may rely on expertise from an external provider such as the vendor or an external consultant, or you may need support from your change champions who will be early adopters and advocates for the planned changes ahead. Sometimes the change team members are able to develop and/or deliver the training; at other times the role of the change practitioners is to prepare or reformat the material provided by the subject matter experts in a user-friendly way. This usually translates to Quick Reference Guides, user support materials, and other visually enhanced user material.

💡 **GOOD TO KNOW**

Hand over to 'Business as Usual': On project-driven change initiatives, the change consultants usually roll off the project just after implementation. After implementation, new people who join the business units will need documentation or learning they can access, to learn how to do their jobs. The change plan or the learning plan needs to consider the collateral that will be handed over to the impacted business units and how this knowledge transfer will take place, so there is continued performance support available. On the list of the change readiness checklist items, there is often an action to remind the project team and the business users to ensure that learning collateral is handed over to the business so they have documentation on processes and information to train new starters.

RELATED CHAPTERS: Change planning, Change impact assessments, Change champions, Change costs

The impact assessment helps you *begin with the end in mind*. It uncovers the skills, behaviours, processes and technology required to support the future state that helps plan training with that end view in mind. #changeessentials

CHANGE COSTS

In the early phases of change planning, the change lead - or on smaller projects, the change consultant - is often asked to evaluate the costs of implementing the change activity. If you are not asked to make an estimate, do it anyway so there are no surprises. This will avoid the risk of being told later that there isn't sufficient budget to implement your change plan or engage the resources you need. Include an outline of the estimated change costs in your change plan.

While each project or initiative will have varied requirements that will incur specific or unique costs, there are common expenses for change managers to consider.

GETTING STARTED

When you have a good idea of your planned change activity, take some time to list all the associated costs. You may want to brainstorm this with other project team members. To anticipate costs, consider what is actually changing, and the high-level impacts. It can be easy to overlook the obvious without the wisdom of others.

To make sure all possible expenses are considered, I find it helpful to sort the costs into two categories:

1 | Change Activity

2 | Impact Type.

COSTS CONSIDERATIONS BY TYPICAL CHANGE ACTIVITIES:

Change Activity	Considerations
Change implementation	Recruitment of external resources: change, training, communication, instructional designers, organisational design specialists, etc.
Stakeholder engagement	Journey mapping.
	Developing employee and/or customer personas.
	Online survey subscriptions, eg SurveyMonkey.
	Expos, project showcases, venue hire.
Communications	Branding.
	Printing of collateral, banners, posters.
	WebEx subscriptions, intranet or website development.
	Visual management, eg mobile whiteboards.
	Purchase of images for image library.
	Videography.
	Podcasting equipment.
Learning and performance support	Printing.
	Other training resources: flipchart paper, post-it notes, markers, adhesive putty, flipchart stands, etc.
	eLearning - licences, development.
	Support from change champions and/or Subject Matter Experts (SME) - time cost to business unit.
	Logistics: hire of training rooms, facilities.
	Catering.
	Travel: airfares, taxis, accommodation, meals, other out-of-pocket expenses related to travel.

Change Activity	Considerations
Change champions and super users	Travel.
	Catering for meetings, workshops.
	Time charged to project.
Business readiness	Online survey subscriptions.
	Legal consultation.
Board engagement	Printing of reading material, postage.
	Logistics, catering.
Engagement with industry bodies or Trade Unions	Industry memberships and subscriptions.
	Conference attendance.
	Travel to meetings, etc.
Organisational design	Organisational design specialist/s
Other	Project team milestones, celebrations and rewards, catering.

COSTS CONSIDERATIONS BY IMPACT TYPES

Impact Type	
People	Project go-live kits/welcome, eg chocolate bars etc, to celebrate implementation.
	Training.
Process	Process documentation, eg from vendor.
Technology	Licences.
	Computer hardware and software.
	Training environments, test beds.
Customer	Communication to external customers – mail.
	Brochures and other marketing collateral, forms.
	Website updates.

These tables cover most of the change costs you are likely to encounter. There are change initiatives that incur rather unique expenses. For example, when working on an Employee Experience Program, I recommended a three-dimensional, visual project wall and walk-through area that would attract attention and act as a gathering place for stakeholder engagement. In this area, we included budget for mannequins that we could dress up as our three employee personas. Now, that definitely attracted attention and sparked some productive conversations!

Document your expected costs in a table in your change plan. If you are working on a smaller or agile project where your plan appears as a *change on a page*, prepare this as a separate document to discuss with your Program or Project Leader to seek budget approval.

SHOWING COST ESTIMATES

Once you have identified all the costs associated with delivering the change plan, you will need to prepare cost estimates. In this activity, it's useful to show it in two parts:

1 | People-related costs - the cost of engaging people resources as part of the project

2 | Non-people related costs.

CHANGE MANAGEMENT ESTIMATE TABLE

Here's an example of a change management estimate with expected effort, activity duration and cost, which can be included in the change management plan. When a change manager is involved in the very early phase of the project, these estimates may appear in earlier documentation such as the Business Case.

PEOPLE RESOURCES:

Change Activity	Resource	Expected Effort	Activity Start Date	Activity End Date	Cost
All change activity	Change Manager	X days x $ cost per day	Month & year	Month & year	$
	Change Analyst				
Communications	Communications Manager				
Learning and performance support	Instructional Designer				

OTHER (NON-PEOPLE RESOURCE COSTS):

Change Activity	Details	Cost	Unit	Total
Marketing collateral	Purpose, description			
Learning collateral				
Travel				
Milestones/celebrations				
Customer collateral				
Town Halls and other engagement events				
Surveys				
Catering				
Software licences				
eLearning/webinars				
Enterprise social networks				
Printing, stationery for workshops, visual management				

It's prudent to add a 5-10% contingency to your estimate, to accommodate price rises and unexpected activity. Clearly stating an activity start and an activity end date places you in a better position to request more budget if timelines are moved or extended.

According to the Change First White Paper, *ROI for Change Management*, the funds allocated to change management comprise, on average, 15% of the project budget.

♟ GOOD TO KNOW

Remember, not all change initiatives are the same. Each organisation and change type will carry its own nuances and risks that may require different or additional expenses to those identified here.

RELATED CHAPTERS: Change planning

16

CHANGE MEASURES

Why do we have change activities, and how do we know if they are effective?

To ensure we transition our impacted users smoothly from the current state to the future environment, we need to understand if our change activities are hitting the mark, and refine our planned activity accordingly. A change plan often identifies the change objectives and the measures of change success. Depending on the type of change initiative, the plan will detail indicators of success measures such as adoption rates, behaviours, user feedback and process efficiencies.

It's important to highlight these measures, as they demonstrate the value of change management, with insights into what may happen if the change activities were not undertaken. For example, if we introduce a new system and training has not occurred in time for implementation, we can expect user adoption to be slow and capability to be low. As stakeholders may often ask about success measures or success of change adoption, you can point them to this section of your change plan.

A word of caution here is that the change practitioner is not responsible for delivering the business benefits of the program of work or the project. When identifying and documenting change measures, make sure they are directly related to the planned change initiatives and not the overall project implementation deliverables.

GETTING STARTED

Here's an approach to get started:

1 | Look at each change activity planned for the project

2 | Identify which of these activities will be measured

3 | Consider measures for each activity - are they qualitative or quantitative?

4 | When will the activity be measured in the project life cycle? Before implementation or after implementation?

5 | Do you need to set 'targets' for each measure?

6 | Document these in your change plan

7 | Seek agreement from your project manager

8 | Consider:
    a.   How will the data for the metrics be collected?
    b.   How will the data be reported? How often? What will it look like?
    c.   Who will receive the information? Who needs to know? How will it be shared?

There are a few ways you can represent this in your change plan. One commonly used method is to list the key change activities and their associated measures of success. Here's an example in a table:

Change Activity / Success Element	Success Measures	When Measured
Leadership and business ownership	Leaders model new behaviours and mindset to support the change.	During transition and post
	Leaders help their teams make sense of the change.	Throughout project lifecycle

Change Activity / Success Element	Success Measures	When Measured
Communications and engagement	Intranet site visits and unique visitors. Enterprise Social Network group members and engagement levels.	Throughout project lifecycle
Learning and development	90% impacted users attended training. X% evaluated training positively with an average rating of 4 out of 5.	During training period
Change champions	Change champions are reporting back on issues and engagement. X% change champions/super users available for hypercare* support.	From change champion program kick-off Post-implementation
Hypercare and performance support	Adherence to hypercare guidelines at and post go-live. All hypercare groups understand their support model and their role and service level agreements. All impacted user groups are using self-serve support options - eg Quick Reference Guides. X% positive response on questions in Change Readiness Survey.	Pre- and post-implementation

 GOOD TO KNOW

What is hypercare? *Hypercare is the elevated level of support provided just after go-live, typically after a systems implementation. This addresses the increase in support required and promotes confidence in and adoption of the new system. Hypercare may be a dedicated help-line, online chat services and/or the presence of super users to provide on-site assistance.

AFTER IMPLEMENTATION

The nature of many change initiatives is project based. This means that change team members are usually rolled off the project just after implementation, or after the hypercare period, so we are not always there to see the fruits of our work. For this reason, it's a good idea to identify change measures before implementation and while the change activities are underway, as indicators of engagement. To continue embedding the change, hand over ownership of post-implementation measures to the business owners.

MEASURING DEEPER ENGAGEMENT

Another change measurement approach I've used more recently is through the lens of human-centred design (HCD). Whilst the concept of HCD is often applied for developing personas and building empathy for our customers, the same thinking can be used to introduce change and measure its benefits. In this approach, we consider our impacted employees as our internal customers who can provide deep insights. With this lens we can look at these three elements *before* and *after* the implementation:

1 | What do we want our people to *DO?*

2 | What do we want them to *THINK?*

3 | What do we want them to *FEEL?*

Taking this approach sends a clear message that we've not only considered the metrics early in our planning, but that our success measures also have a human-centric focus.

Gather input from your impacted employees. Ask them what they see themselves doing, how they want to feel, and what they want to think after implementation. We are inviting them to play a meaningful role in imagining a successful future state. This involvement through *future-pacing* prepares people for the change, with visual imagery. It engages them in what success looks like, giving them a positive view of the new world. The key benefit for change practitioners is that we gain insights into what a desired future state looks like from a user's perspective.

HUMAN CENTRIC METRICS
DOING-THINKING-FEELING

WHAT TO DO BEFORE IMPLEMENTATION		WHAT TO MEASURE AFTER IMPLEMENTATION
ACTIVITY		**INDICATORS**
① Post a visual dashboard with progress		① Speed of adoption, e.g. logins, queries to service
① Align metrics in performance scorecards	**DOING**	desk, site visits
① Provide training & performance support		① Leaders are role modelling
		① Feedback from super users & coaches
① Run discussion forums		① Feedback from change network
① Promote dialogue on ESNs		
① Co-create the future state		① ESN dialogue & engagement
① Run retrospectives	**THINKING**	
① Remove artefacts of the old culture		① Lessons learned through retrospectives
① Coach & support		
① Agree on follow up approaches		① Pulse check surveys
① Gather feedback anonymously		① Anecdotal feedback
① Run change readiness surveys	**FEELING**	① Observation
① Remove artefacts of the old		① Testimonials
① culture		
① Collect & retell success stories		

© Lena Ross, 2016

This image can be downloaded as a colour infographic from my website.

DISPLAY YOUR METRICS

If you've noticed large billboards displaying fundraising activity and how it's progressing using visual icons such as barometers, you understand the effectiveness of visually displaying metrics. Our attention spans seem to be shorter, and as a result we are seeing an increasing amount of data displayed in a visual format, often in a *dashboard* format. In a later chapter on communicating to co-create, I talk about the power of visual communication.

For infographics, you can easily find icons in slide templates, or purchase icon images that can be used many times. Your organisation may have an icon library you can use. Simply google 'infographics' and you will find numerous examples of how data has been represented, with use of colour, layout and icons to get you inspired. Once you have created a template with colours that align to your branding palette, you are on your way to designing visually compelling messages and a dashboard.

To convey powerful messages and promote engagement, update your metrics that show growth in numbers or percentage regularly and in real time. A great deal of research suggests that when we can easily see our progress towards goals, we are more likely to stay motivated and engaged.

The change roadmap discussed in the chapter on change planning is a form of infographic that visually shows key activity and dates.

MISALIGNED METRICS

Sometimes metrics may concentrate so much on one area that they overlook other behaviours or adverse impacts that may result from such focus.

A classic example used by MIT is Continental Airlines recovering from bankruptcy in the 1990s. Continental Airlines had to cut costs, and because fuel costs were high, management created a metric to track its usage. They used this metric to reward pilots for reducing fuel consumption. As expected, pilots acted to earn their reward - they skimped on air conditioning and flew more slowly. Management got what they wanted, it seemed, and fuel consumption fell. Unexpectedly, however, their customer satisfaction and on-time performance also fell due to delays and late arrivals. Their most valuable frequent flyer customers moved on to competitors.

More recently, the Banking Royal Commission Inquiry in Australia uncovered that a great deal of the misconduct was driven by employee performance metrics and rewards.

The adjustments that need to be made in performance scorecards, so they align with the change effort, are often overlooked. Beware of misaligned or absent metrics. Involve the business users in developing the measures by asking, 'What does success look like to you?'. Check that your measures support and reward the *desired* changes in the way people think, behave and practise.

RELATED CHAPTERS: Change planning, Making change stick, Project management and change management, Communicate to co-create, Change champions

Whilst human-centred design principles are often applied for developing personas and building empathy for our customers, the same thinking can be used to introduce change and measure its benefits. #changeessentials

Sometimes metrics focus so much on one area that they can overlook other behaviours or adverse impacts that may result from such focus. #changeessentials

17

MAKING CHANGE STICK

By now, you've read about the core change capabilities, along with change measures. Some of you may be thinking more deeply about the role you play in getting other people on board and embedding new behaviours and practices, especially when working on programs that involve culture change and new ways of working.

The best-intended change plans can miss the element of *making the change stick.* Embedding the change to ensure it becomes part of the organisational DNA calls for some planning in itself. To land the change initiative successfully, we need to create an environment where the people receiving the change, often called *change receivers,* feel empowered to continually improve their business. These end users need to feel comfortable integrating new approaches in their day-to-day practice.

Your change plan is an opportunity to highlight the factors that help shift and sustain new approaches, to support the benefits realisation. Your proposed change activity that will support and embed the new ways can be identified in your handover plan.

Let's explore how you can make an impact or make recommendations in your change plan to shift mindsets and behaviours - aka the culture!

MAKING IT STICK

To make change stick, consider the four elements that address individual, team and organisational levels:

1 | **Model** what you want others to think, act and do

2 | **Recruit** the right people

3 | **Reward** the right mindset and behaviours

4 | **Reinforce** what you want to see repeated and embedded.

1. MODEL IT

Whether impacted users or change champions have direct reports or not, we can't underestimate the impact that each person's behaviour has on those around them. From studies on primal human behaviour, we know that how we act is observed, absorbed and easily mimicked by others, making it critical that the desired behaviour is modelled.

This sounds straightforward, yet too often leaders miss this simple way of influencing others and get it wrong. You would be surprised at what I've seen in my many years of working in and consulting to organisations. By way of just a couple of examples, I've seen the leader who:

- Advocates collaborative workspace/hot desking practices while claiming a desk of their own
- Communicates a rule that there are no mobile phones in meetings, yet they bring theirs because they are expecting an 'important' call
- Arrives late to meetings, consistently, and expresses impatience when waiting for others
- Speaks to team members with little or no eye contact, while looking around the room or looking elsewhere.

I'm sure you have numerous examples to add to this list. The 'do as I say, not what I do' approach is too prevalent.

A good message for senior leaders is to be aware of the subtle messages they may be sending. These types of *status signals* communicate arrogance, demotivate teams and can sabotage efforts for behaviour change. We are probably all guilty of doing things we are not particularly proud of, consciously or unconsciously, as part of our learning. The key message here is to be mindful of your own actions as the change practitioner.

Keep in mind that we are always modelling behaviours - consciously and unconsciously - and the people around us will copy us at a subconscious level. The ripple effect of how we act has a significant impact on what others will do.

2. RECRUIT THE RIGHT PEOPLE

When successful change relies on shifts in mindset and behaviours, recruitment will need to focus on the right fit to support the new culture. If you need to call in selection expertise, it usually involves engaging your Human Resources business partner to discuss realigning recruitment approaches to source the right people. This will need a clear definition of the desired behaviours so an appropriate search process and set of interview questions are established to attract and find the right talent. Ideally you will search and find the behaviours and capabilities required to support the change.

Previous experience alone is not a reliable indicator. Experience and skills do not guarantee that somebody has the mindset and behaviours you want. To help you identify the people you want on your team, the interview questions you ask need to uncover the alignment. A couple of questions to get you started could sound like this:

- What did you like most about the last project you worked on?
- Tell me about a challenge you experienced when working with the team? And what you did about it?
  Use the behavioural interviewing approach to hear about real examples where your potential team members can describe the situation, what they actually did and the outcome. To gather more information, probe a little further and ask:
- Then what happened?
- What did you learn from that?

3. REWARD IT

One organisation I worked in invested a great deal of time and money developing their new 'corporate values'. Cascading from those values was a statement of the behaviours they wanted to cultivate. Out rolled the roadshow to spread the word, along with glossy, colour posters and business-card size pocket cards so we could all have them at our fingertips. How successful was this approach? Did the behaviours change? Did the change stick?

Sadly, no it didn't. One very simple element was overlooked. The behaviours were not clearly defined. There were no rewards for demonstrating them, or consequences for *not* demonstrating them. As a disclaimer, I must mention that this occurred in the days before I was a change practitioner, but I did ask why we were not being measured and rewarded on something that appeared to be important to the organisation.

Once you, or the Human Resources team or Change Sponsor, have identified the actions that demonstrate the mindset and behaviours needed to support the change initiative, define them clearly. You may need examples to make the definitions easy to understand. Examples could range from exemplary behaviours to those less desired to showcase the contrast of what is good and not so good.

These are the definitions that need to form part of the organisation's reward and performance program and appear in employee performance scorecards and capability statements as desired behaviours. Once they land in the performance program, you can reward what you want to see.

4. REINFORCE AND EMBED IT

Okay, you have the first three recommendations ticked off. You've flagged modelling the right behaviours, aligning the recruitment approach to get the *right people on the bus*, and setting up your organisation's performance program to reward the teams and individuals who are on board and demonstrating the capabilities to support the change.

There is one more element to cover off: to see the desired behaviours repeated and embedded, so they become *the way we do things around here*. To reinforce is to repeatedly remind your people what you like to see in your organisation. You can use a few different approaches to get the message across:

- Make the examples of great behaviour public through stories that appear on the corporate intranet and enterprise social networks
- Encourage people to nominate team members whom they see doing the right thing, with a reward system in place for the nominees

- Set up a Kudos Board for your own team, where other team members can post notes on who they've seen demonstrate exemplary behaviour and what they did. How cool is it to see your own name in a public place when you least expect it?

Embedding the right stuff is a result of repeatedly *modelling* it, *recruiting* it and *rewarding* it.

💡 GOOD TO KNOW

Once the change has been implemented and the project closed out, as the dedicated change practitioner, you're typically rolled off that initiative quite quickly. If you're an external contractor, you're likely to finish up and leave the organisation to pick up your next gig. If you're an internal employee, you will be moved on to the next project to ensure they you are fully utilised. Who is around to make sure the change is handed over effectively to the change receivers? Who makes sure the change sticks? Make sure you have covered this in your change plan and your handover plan.

I'll wrap up this chapter with one of my favourite quotes, often attributed to Peter Drucker:

What is important is measured

What is measured is done

What is done is rewarded

What is rewarded is repeated

You might even want to use this quote in your change plan. This is where the rubber really hits the ground - sounds like a good change management approach to me!

RELATED CHAPTERS: Change planning, Change measures, Psychological safety

The best intended change plans can miss the element of how to make the change stick. #changeessentials

18

CHANGE MYTHS

You will hear myths and sweeping statements in your travels as a change consultant. There are many assumptions which are not quite true, so unleash your curiosity and validate what is often accepted as truth.

Here are a few of my favourite myths for you to ponder:

MYTH 1: 70% OF CHANGE EFFORTS FAIL

I once believed this myself. And I am guilty of quoting this statistic in change plans to build the 'case for change management'. Then, as part of my MBA, I chose Change Management as one of my elective subjects. Everyone thought it was a soft option for me as I was already working as a change consultant at the time. But I didn't want to formally study change to have an easy semester. In fact, I'm sure my lecturer was twice as hard on me for disclosing my true occupation! I genuinely wanted to discover what was being taught as 'best practice' in educational institutions and dive into case studies as part of group discussions.

And so the real learning began. In my major paper, I wanted to mention that 70% of change efforts are not successful. For all university papers, almost every sentence you write needs to be attributed, footnoted, and annotated. Imagine my surprise when I couldn't find a credible source for this.

A couple of years later, I was introduced to Dr Jen Frahm, and her article *70% of change projects fail: Bollocks*. This online article delves into the *unscientific* statements of change success that have led to widespread acceptance of the myth as we continue to see the 70% figure quoted in articles, including in well-regarded publications such as *Harvard Business Review*. Yet the sources quoted, if at all, remain flimsy.

The article highlights good reasons to re-think the 70% claim, including the importance of how 'success' and 'change projects' are defined, and when success is actually measured. After reading Dr Jen Frahm's full article (which you can easily find it on her *Conversations of Change* website), I encourage you to run a simple google search on 'challenging 70% of change efforts fail' to uncover other thought-provoking articles on this topic by well-respected change professionals such as Gail Severini, Jason Little and Heather Stagl. Also, it's worth checking out the original 2011 academic article on this, written by Mark Hughes in the *Journal of Change Management*. In his article, Hughes raised awareness of the lack of empirical evidence to support this widely held belief.

MYTH 2: PEOPLE NATURALLY RESIST CHANGE

There's a generally held assumption that people don't like change, that change is hard, or that humans naturally resist change.

Numerous change models are dedicated to explaining resistance, resistance cycles and linear approaches to 'manage' resistance. The reality is that humans, and their responses, are rarely linear or predictable. Change management training sessions often talk about resistance without acknowledging that it is only one of many responses to change.

Too many change plans start with the assumption that there will be resistance to change. I kick off conversations about responses to change by introducing the human paradox about our evolution.

The human paradox

We humans are wired to resist change in some instances, yet embrace it at other times. This may sound confusing, but if we wholeheartedly disliked change, how could we be the most adaptable species on the planet? Why did we bother to venture out of the trees, roam the savannah, walk upright, diversify our diet, and eventually manipulate many aspects of our natural environment, yet be likely to resist the introduction of a new system or structure at work?

Resistance is one of many responses to change. This is explored in greater detail in my chapters on Change Resistance and Brain-Friendly Change.

MYTH 3: CHANGE MANAGERS ARE CHANGE LEADERS

In the time I've spend studying change management, both formally at university and informally through on-the-job experience, I've noticed that there is a widespread misunderstanding of the difference between *change leadership* and *change management*. Some of the confusion may be due to the assignment of job titles such as *change lead* to change practitioners.

Change leadership and change management are two different roles that complement another. To demonstrate this in my workshops, I use the metaphor of two oval-shaped magnetic rocks. When the two magnetic rocks are apart, there is no traction or energy. When you throw them together, they meet and create a noticeable buzz. It's like this with change: the change leaders need change managers to help make it happen, and vice versa.

More recently, Dr Jen Frahm has used the brilliant analogy of rock stars and roadies to highlight the difference. Our change leaders are the rock stars, who are front and centre. They are the voice and face of the organisation leading the change initiative, and often the change sponsor. The change managers support the change leaders, or rock stars, as their roadies. Like it or not, we need to make this distinction: change practitioners are the roadies, not the rock stars.

I've been engaged in numerous discussions with change practitioners who disagree and insist that they are 'leading' the change. The confusion appears to come from the fact that many change managers are effective influencers. It's true that strong influencing skills demonstrate admirable leadership, but in the context of delivering change, the change manager is not the change leader. The two roles require different sets of capabilities and purpose.

Another way to clarify the confusion is to watch John Kotter's YouTube clip called *The Key Differences Between Leading and Managing,* along with a clip produced by Kotter International titled *Change Management versus Change Leadership.* In the context of change initiatives and activity, here's the distinction between the two roles:

CHANGE
LEADERSHIP v MANAGEMENT

CHANGE LEADERSHIP STRATEGIC FOCUS	CHANGE MANAGEMENT OPERATIONAL FOCUS
	Draws on tools, processes & practices to create a change plan to support the vision
Creates vision for the future	
Selects steering committee to support new vision	Enables change largely through change methods & tools
Delivers key messages to inspire & motivate people	Creates the communication plan for leaders to deliver
Escalates risks & issues to remove obstacles	Plans, manages & responds to change requirements. Identifies risks & issues
Endorses recommendations for new performance measures	Recommends performance & success measures for the future state

MYTH 4: CHANGE MANAGEMENT IS DEAD

You may see this idea floating around in articles and posts. As a statement on its own, the claim is causing some alarm and confusion in the change community. Firstly, let's look at the reality, some of which may have led to this assumption.

The reality: Change is changing, so the nature of our work is evolving and demanding new capabilities. The term 'change management' may become obsolete as we do not really 'manage' change.

But... Change managers, performing the role under many possible titles, will continue to advise leaders and sponsors on how to support their people through the change, for optimal adoption and productivity.

Our skills can be honed if we have an open mindset and commitment to continuous learning. Change practitioners who themselves don't want to change, adapt or learn new ways will be less relevant and valuable. Leaders will continue to 'lead change'.

The message is clear: stay ahead of the curve and keep learning to stay future-fit as a change consultant.

What is questionable?

A couple of the protagonists on this topic even use the *70% of change efforts fail* myth as a reason to support the notion that change management as an occupation is waning. Fancy that - using one myth to support another!

Although we hear that change management is dead, a great deal of literature reminds us of the highly visible and relentless pace of change. It's quite clear that the role of the change specialist will become even more valued and in demand by organisations, so rather than saying that change management is dead, it makes more sense to say that change is changing. This is why I've dedicated an entire section in this book - *A brave new world* - to explaining the practitioner's role in the changing nature of change management.

MYTH 5: CHANGE MANAGEMENT IS JUST COMMUNICATIONS AND TRAINING

There's a myth that change management is simply about delivering communications and training. Clearly, this is an indicator that in many circles change management remains misunderstood.

This myth may have stemmed from early change management practice, or from the way that many smaller-scale business-as-usual process changes are implemented, and possibly from various other sources. Like all urban myths, this one is fictional and of obscure origin, so it's time to explode it with the reality!

We know it isn't true that change management is just communications and training. It's up to us, the change practitioners, to continue to dispel this myth through the work we do.

RELATED CHAPTERS: Change sponsorship, Change communications, Change impact assessment, Change measures

Change is changing, so the nature of our work is evolving and demanding new capabilities. #changeessentials

Change practitioners who themselves don't want to change, adapt or learn new ways will be less relevant and valuable. #changeessentials

#

It makes more sense to say 'change is changing' rather than 'change management is dead'. #changeessentials

19

CHANGE CHAMPIONS

Long before I worked in change management, and possibly before change was defined as a dedicated occupation, I remember sitting in my manager's office in my role as an airline duty manager. We were discussing the introduction of a new service policy to cabin crew, and on her whiteboard was one word - *zealots*. I knew what a zealot was but was not sure why it was written up there in big capital letters, so I asked.

My manager was a very progressive leader with excellent engagement skills, and this was the first time I was exposed to the power of leveraging change champions. Almost every change plan references or considers a change champion network. Depending on the type of change initiative, these people are your mavens, influencers, raving fans, early adopters, evangelists or super users.

WHY WE NEED OUR CHANGE CHAMPIONS

The purpose of building a change champion network is to promote and encourage an understanding of the change, and minimise disruption and impacts by embedding change advocates across the organisation.

Change champions establish and maintain a link between the business and the project to support implementation activities, provide go-live support, and act as an ongoing means of transfer of knowledge to the business. Champions are familiar with the nuances and day-to-day operations of their own business units, so they can identify and address small obstacles before they become bigger blockers to the success of the change initiative.

The main objectives of the change champion network are to:

- Provide subject matter expertise with input to and review of change deliverables, such as impact assessment, learning materials and testing
- Encourage commitment to and adoption of the change, uptake of new technologies, processes and/or behaviours
- Communicate information to their business units and peers, with consideration to preferences and nuances within their own teams
- Provide change mentoring and coaching to impacted users
- Play back sentiments on change readiness and change acceptance within their business unit
- Be available 'on the ground' to promote changes and address questions and concerns, to enable a more informed workforce
- Provide post go-live support.

We know that successful change is business-led rather than project-led, and a change champion network brings a strong people-centric lens to engagement and adoption.

FINDING YOUR CHAMPIONS

There are various ways to find your change champions, depending on the organisation and whether there is a preferred approach to uncover them.

Change champions can be nominated by their leaders or peers. They often do not hold senior role titles; rather, they are well respected in the business and are able to exercise informal power as agents of change.

Don't forget to look beyond the formal hierarchy and the stakeholder matrix to find your enthusiastic ravers and the quiet achievers who are hidden influencers in the organisation through their ability to enable, connect and network. When you mention their name, you'll hear words of respect or admiration and very rarely anything negative about them. They are usually as competent in their job role as they are at building their social capital and personal brand.

If you have an enterprise social networking channel such as *Yammer* or *Slack* in your organisation, take a look at the users with a strong, yet positive voice. They have lots of followers. They post frequently to various groups. They invite comment, offer interesting insights and help connect people across the organisation when they identify a mutual need or goal. Other users are weighing-in, commenting on and sharing their posts. When I needed to kick off a social learning initiative a few years ago, it was the *Yammer* influencers who helped me launch and drive the program across the organisation through their support and involvement.

Sometimes the change champion self-nominates by responding to a call for supporters. This is common where a large number of advocates are needed to support the change initiative.

CHARACTERISTICS

A change champion is typically:
- Well networked within the organisation and respected by peers
- Seen as a go-to person who is able to influence others
- Confident to represent their business unit's issues and concerns
- Enthusiastic to represent the change within the business
- Approachable and accessible
- A good communicator and listener
- Equipped with a good understanding of their own business area and its cultural nuances.

CHANGE CHAMPION NETWORK BRIEFING

Once you have identified your bunch of supporters, schedule a briefing session to set expectations and provide an opportunity for them to meet each other. In the session, cover these points:

- Project purpose, key activities and milestones
- Business benefits
- What's in it for them
- Org chart showing project team members and their roles
- Why they were chosen
- Champion role expectations and activities
- Specific time commitment across the project lifecycle. - consider the peak periods close to implementation dates
- Thank them for their contribution and acknowledge the importance of their role
- Where to find additional project information, including key messages, frequently asked questions and talking points - these could be in a shared folder that can be accessed via the intranet
- How you will communicate with them moving forward
- A key point of contact for change champion network members.

WORKING TOGETHER

Throughout the change program, there are many ways to stay connected and work together with your change champions. It's a good idea to ask them in the initial briefing how they'd like to remain connected as a group.

Encourage peer-to-peer collaboration within the network. In change champion networks I've built, I've found this approach helps establish cross-business unit networks that continue beyond the life cycle of the project. Some have established their own groups on ESNs, such as *Yammer* and *Slack*, to share ideas, experiences and challenges.

WIN/WIN OUTCOMES

Change champions often take on the role in addition to their day-to-day responsibilities. As most champions are enthusiastic agents of change, it's unlikely you will need to convince them with the benefits of participating in the network.

However, there are change champion network benefits for the individuals *and* the business, resulting in win/win outcomes, which are worth mentioning in champion briefings and documentation:

Business Benefits	Individual Benefits
• Builds commitment to the change from people whom team members know and trust	• Develops skills in change management and coaching
• Accelerates acceptance and adoption	• Builds personal profile and visibility in the business as an early adopter and change agent
• Builds capability within the business with super users	• Acknowledges contribution and effort in performance conversations
• Opens another channel to communicate to the business	• Provides an opportunity to positively contribute to a change program and participate in a range of activities such to impact assessments, training design and delivery
• Provides early identification of sentiment and issues through a trusted feedback loop	
• Ensures that the solution meets the business requirements	

Remember that your sponsor is your number one change champion; and hopefully your stakeholders are all advocates too.

⚡ GOOD TO KNOW

The difference between a change champion and a super user: On larger projects, especially large-scale technology implementations, the roles of *change champion* and *super user* may be separate from each other. On smaller projects, the same person often carries out both roles.

What is a change champion?

- A change champion is often an impacted employee who represents the typical user.

- The change champion is a change ambassador, who acts as the key driver by providing essential input to successfully manage impacted employees through the change curve via regular two-way communication and support.

What is a super user?

- A super user is focused on the application of a new system or approach, and provides process support for users in the go-live and post-go-live period, often referred to as hypercare.

Change champions support delivery and implementation, as they play a key role in adoption in many capacities - as behaviour models, coaches, trainers, experts, or first points of contact. They are your ears and eyes on the ground. Find them, nurture them and reward them for their contribution to your change initiative.

RELEVANT CHAPTERS: Change planning, Stakeholder engagement, Learning and performance support

We know that successful change is business-led rather than project-led, and a change champion network brings a strong people-centric lens to engagement and adoption. #changeessentials

Encourage peer-to-peer collaboration within your change champion network. This approach helps establish cross-business unit networks that continue beyond the life cycle of the project. #changeessentials

20

CHANGE READINESS

Imagine this scenario. You are moving house. Your removalist provides you with some handy hints on moving. Somewhere in there, you will probably find a checklist to ensure you have advised the right people of your new address, turned services off, activated services to your new address, that recommend what to pack first and what to pack last, and so on. The overall goal is to improve your experience so you settle more quickly, and to minimise disruption to your essential services and utilities. This is similar to completing a change readiness checklist.

DEFINITION

Change readiness broadly refers to activity that is designed to check or assess the readiness of the business and its people, to implement and adopt the planned change. It's a way to check that everything is in place so end users are ready for the change. This includes documented policies and procedures, business rules, new role descriptions, access to systems, skills uplift and post-implementation support.

The change plan typically documents the change readiness approach with details on the planned activities that will be carried out, to successfully prepare the impacted employees for the change.

There are two types of change readiness activity:

1 | Change Readiness Checklist

2 | Change Readiness Assessment.

1. CHANGE READINESS CHECKLIST

Just like the 'moving house' checklist, a *change readiness checklist* or questionnaire is primarily carried out to confirm that the impacted end users are ready for 'implementation' or 'go-live' and that change activities have been completed.

This assessment is sometimes called a *business readiness checklist*.

The change practitioner customises the checklist for each change that is to be delivered. As a starting point, your organisation may have a library of questions or checklist items, often sorted in the themes of people, technology, process and customer.

Why complete it?

It provides an overview of *what* activity needs to be completed, for *which audience* at a *specific point in time*, to ensure the business is ready for the change. It may also be used to determine a GO/NO GO decision for a go-live of a systems implementation.

When to complete it

The change readiness checklist is a pre-go-live activity, typically completed in the weeks leading up to the implementation for each stakeholder group.

What it may look like

In this scenario, the checklist is specific to the introduction of a new Point of Sale (POS) system in retail stores:

Impacted Team: Retail Stores			
Activity	**Due date**	**Business Owner**	**Business Ready YES or NO?**
Log on instructions, link and user support instructions communicated to all users			
Online training completed by 80% users			
Quick Reference Guides issued			
Business impacts noted and addressed			
User readiness survey results accepted			
Go-live communications ready, including instructions for Day One			
Store Manager roles and responsibilities clear and communicated			
Change champions briefed and ready			
Performance support and help line numbers set up, tested and communicated			
Ready to accept the change		*One owner*	**YES or NO**

In this scenario, the checklist is presented as a questionnaire; this is a generic readiness questionnaire that can be customised and used by the project team members as part of their engagement with stakeholder groups and/or in team discussions:

Activity	**Business Ready YES or NO?**	**Action Required**
Purpose: *Have we ensured that our key stakeholders and impacted groups understand the reason for the change and the business benefits?*		
Leadership: *Do our business leaders know how to support the change and model aligned behaviours?*		
Engagement: *Have we effectively engaged all impacted business areas throughout the change process? And do they agree that we have done this?*		
Impact Management: *Have we identified all impacts to people, customer, process and technology, and carried out activities to address these impacts?*		

Activity	Business Ready YES or NO?	Action Required
Communications: *Have we developed and distributed key messages, and effectively communicated the timing, nature and impact of the change?*		
Learning: *Have we developed and implemented training activity to address the capability needed to transition from the 'as is' to the 'to be' state; and is an ongoing learning plan in place?*		
Risks: *Have we identified the change risks and devised an action plan to mitigate these risks?*		
Management support: *Have we actively engaged managers and change champions throughout the project to monitor change awareness, commitment, acceptance and readiness?*		
Organisational alignment: *Have we engaged with Human Resources to assess and ensure organisational alignment (organisational/role design, performance/ metrics, pay, etc) to support the end state?*		
Process: *Have we identified and updated relevant supporting operational processes and documentation (eg policy, process, knowledge management, business continuity/disaster recovery plans, post-implementation support model)?*		
BaU handover: *Have we transitioned the change effectively to the Business as Usual (BaU) function (eg help desk knowledge, ownership of learning/user guide materials)?*		
Measurement: *Do we have effective metrics to track change adoption?*		

As mentioned, the checklist contents need to be customised for each change initiative. A change readiness checklist for an office relocation will look very different to one for a system implementation.

2. CHANGE READINESS ASSESSMENT

The *change readiness assessment* is a questionnaire or survey, often carried out at agreed points throughout the project lifecycle, to assess and adjust change activities as required. The objective is to help people escalate their commitment to the change. This is often represented as movement along the change commitment curve from *little or no awareness* to *high levels of engagement* and *commitment*.

When carrying out a change readiness assessment, seek agreement from your project team on:

- How the survey will be carried out, eg Survey Monkey. Remember that this is likely to incur a subscription cost.
- Timing and frequency: when the survey will take place, in which months, how often
- The resources required to carry out the survey and follow up activity: consider the time needed for survey set up, developing questions, drafting and sending emails, reminder emails, collating results.
- How the survey results will be communicated to stakeholder groups.

The assessment should uncover:

- Stakeholder engagement and progress towards commitment
- Issues, opportunities for improvement and potential resistance
- Whether the change management activity is hitting the mark.

The frequency and nature of the assessment depends on the scale and/ or scope of the project. The purpose of carrying out the assessments at stages in the project is to check the progress of engagement with stakeholder groups and to address any potential gaps with realigned change activity. It provides visibility of change readiness to business leads in each stakeholder group, as they may be able to further support change efforts when needed.

Using the change curve as a readiness indicator

One approach I've used, and seen applied across many organisations, is to align the questions to the stages on Conner's and Patterson's commitment curve, to gauge where on the curve the change receivers are at a given point in time. This means you can measure as you go.

Just like assessment of stakeholder engagement, this curve is often simplified and presented in four stages:

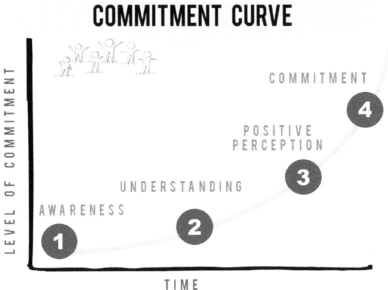

SOURCE: Based on Conner & Patterson Commitment Curve. *Training and Development Journal*, 1982. Vol.36, No.4

The change readiness questions can be designed to specifically evaluate at which stage on the curve the users are, at a point in time. Your change receivers should move upwards on the commitment curve with each progressive assessment.

SURVEY PRACTICES

To get the most out of your survey, with optimal audience participation, keep in mind survey best practice principles, such as:

- Previewing and testing your survey before you send it
- Limiting questions so it takes only 5-10 minutes to complete
- Using simple language
- Assuring confidentiality
- Encouraging participation, so it's voluntary, not mandated.

💡 GOOD TO KNOW

Results from your readiness surveys will uncover useful insights, but the real value and purpose is to drive conversations with your end users and stakeholders.

Keep in mind that change readiness assessments take a great deal of time to be carried out effectively and to deliver value. They are typically used on larger, waterfall projects. Many smaller or agile projects are using pulse check surveys on enterprise social network platforms to gauge how people are feeling and their level of readiness.

Not every change initiative will require a change readiness survey. However, almost all change projects will need a change readiness checklist.

RELEVANT CHAPTERS: Stakeholder engagement

Results from your readiness surveys will uncover useful insights, but the real value and purpose is to drive conversations with your end users and stakeholders. #changeessentials

CHANGE RESISTANCE

Change management training courses often dedicate a great deal of time to exploring why people resist change and how to manage it. Change plans often assume that resistance will occur, and devise a schedule of activities to reduce it.

It's often assumed that we can address resistance by moving people along a change curve, from no awareness of the change to acceptance and commitment. If you've already read the chapter on *Change Myths*, you will know it is my view that resistance is one of many responses to change, and it is not always the default one.

REFRAMING RESISTANCE

As change professionals, when we talk about constructs such as *change resistance* and *change fatigue* (covered in the next chapter), we need to be mindful that we may be signalling through our language that negative emotions are associated with change. Therefore, small shifts in the words we use when we talk about change can make a big difference.

The way we communicate and engage with others, along with the way we absorb incremental change in our personal and professional lives, is accelerating and continually being reshaped. As we are consuming an unprecedented amount of information, it's a good time to closely look at the words we use (or over-use) in change management, and to realign our practice and language to the dynamic nature of the business environment. It's time to nudge, reframe, and yes, challenge the language. In an article I posted on LinkedIn (also on my website) about reframing the language of change, one of the over-used words I challenged was *resistance.*

We need to ask ourselves: *Do we really naturally resist change?* Thanks to recent insights from neuroscience, we now know more about our hard-wired responses and it's time to re-think our assumptions that people will always resist change. For what seems like a long time, when devising our change plans and interventions we've assumed resistance as a starting point, when in fact the human response can range from resistance to support.

The key is to uncover the range of responses, and why reactions to the same change can trigger these varied emotional responses. David Rock's SCARF model eloquently explains the human response to change in terms of loss or gain. Loss equates to threat and gain equates to reward. For each element of SCARF - Status, Certainty, Autonomy, Relatedness and Fairness - our responses to each change that we experience are individual, and can be based on perception alone. There is more content on the SCARF model in a later chapter.

For example, one person can experience a strong emotion to a perceived loss of status that may occur, while another may anticipate gains from an autonomy perspective - for the same change initiative. A starting point of resistance assumes that *all* of our impacted people will experience loss as a result of the change initiative.

DIAGNOSE FIRST...

Let's turn to the timeless mantra of Stephen Covey's seven habits (of highly effective people), and look at habit number 5: *Seek first to understand and then to be understood.* This habit reminds us to listen with empathy, rather than devise a solution through the lens of our own experiences or assumptions – that is, to look at things with a beginner's mindset.

A mindset of 'response' instead of 'resistance' opens the path to deep engagement.

By shifting our frame of reference and language with regard to resistance, we can change the way we approach engagement and create a new capacity for action. Starting with an assumption that there will be a *varied response* helps us plan for deep engagement, through co-creation and collaboration. If we uncover resistance as part of that engagement, we discover it as an outcome rather than an up-front assumption.

In that discovery, we can 'unpack' the emotional response and reason for that resistance. Simply collaborating with our colleagues as early as possible is likely to reduce the level of threat they may feel. Now, that's bound to help us develop a more meaningful approach to see our change land successfully.

This aligns our change planning and approach with the principles of human-centred design, explored more in the last section, *A brave new world*. We can start with the people who will be impacted by the change, build *real empathy* and explore ideas on how to make the change stick, by looking at what our people are *doing*, how they are *thinking* and what they are *feeling*.

WHAT LIES BENEATH?

With continuous, concurrent and rapid change, we are challenged to think about what emotional responses lie beneath a conventional change curve of resistance and adoption. Many change curves assume a starting point of resistance that can be diminished in a linear way, as people move up the curve to adoption, with change management interventions.

I'm not suggesting we discard change models and frameworks that have served us well. I'm proposing we adopt the *beginner's mindset* for each change initiative, where we:

- Don't judge or assume - put aside our own biases and expectations
- Question everything - keep asking why, just as children do
- Are intensely curious
- Look for patterns or themes that emerge among our impacted users.

With a shift in mindset and approach, we can uncover the range of emotional human responses to the change through deep engagement, which will set up our change programs for the best chance of success.

This means the purpose of change management is not solely to minimise resistance. We have an obligation to devise change plans that promote adoption to improve productivity. A dip in productivity does not always represent resistance. When we learn and apply new things, including adopting new practices and behaviours, we experience cognitive load. In turn, this impacts our productivity as we are concentrating on the new task. Once we are capable, our productivity resumes.

THE LINK TO THE BOTTOM LINE

Explaining the productivity dip that occurs with change is an effective way of showing how important it is to carefully plan change and engagement activities when we introduce new approaches in the workplace. This is the people side of 'return on investment'. In fact, it is the explanation I created after being asked by a senior manager, early in my career: *How does change management and the related activities contribute to our bottom line?*

It's an opportunity to explain the *hidden costs* of potential resistance, the sense of threat our people may experience, and the absence of a robust change management plan.

The following diagram shows time on one axis and organisational performance on the other. The business case for the change initiative aspires to realise benefits straight away. But when we introduce change we disrupt the current state, and productivity declines because people need to do something differently. The dip in productivity is a hidden cost to the business. Our goal is to reduce the productivity dip with carefully devised change management activity such as engagement, training and performance support.

THE PRODUCTIVITY DIP

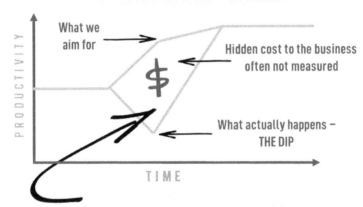

WITH OUR NEW INSIGHTS FROM BRAIN SCIENCE, WE CAN UNPACK WHAT'S GOING ON IN HERE TO UNDERSTAND WHAT PEOPLE ARE EXPERIENCING

SOURCE: Inspired by various change curves that feature the *Valley of Despair*

WHEN YOU IDENTIFY RESISTANCE

There is some truth in the belief that people naturally resist change - it's when they feel they are under threat. A question that I'm often asked is: *Why don't people change when there is an extremely compelling reason to, such as health issues?*

I can only assume that the perceived reward, or enjoyment, of their current lifestyle - such as eating junk food, little exercise, high sugar - outweighs (in their minds) the reward of being healthier. Here's a visual reminder of how we respond to threat and reward:

THREAT AND REWARD

WHEN **THREAT** IS
GREATER
THAN REWARD

RESISTANCE

THREAT > REWARD

WHEN **REWARD** IS
GREATER
THAN THREAT

ACCEPTANCE

REWARD > THREAT

💡 GOOD TO KNOW

When impacted users experience threat in response to a change initiative, expect resistance.

However, when there is perceived reward, you are more likely to see acceptance.

In the chapter on *Brain-friendly change* in the last section, you will find additional information on the SCARF model and ways to reduce the threat response.

RELATED CHAPTERS: Change myths, Brain-friendly change, Change management meets design thinking

#

With a shift in mindset and approach, we can uncover the range of emotional human responses to change through deep engagement, and set up our change programs for the best chance of success. #changeessentials

#

When threat is greater than the reward response, expect resistance. When the reward response outweighs the perceived threat, expect acceptance. #changeessentials

22

CHANGE FATIGUE

Many people will say that when there is a sense of disengagement, cynicism or apathy towards change initiatives, it is because of *change fatigue*. The concept of change fatigue has been circulating for a couple of decades and has been cited as one of the reasons that change efforts fail.

Change fatigue is a term used to describe when an organisation feels stressed or exhausted by the change occurring in their business. This can be the *volume* of change in terms of a great number of change implementations, or the *scope* of change, where one or a few initiatives are intense and far-reaching across the enterprise, or both.

PERCEPTION

The construct of change fatigue is difficult to define because of its subjectivity. What feels like too much change for one person may be an entirely different experience for another. One organisation with a small amount of change may claim change fatigue as an obstacle, and another organisation experiencing continuous change may never mention it.

When you hear the term change fatigue, it's a good idea to investigate it further. Ask: *How much change is too much? And what if there is more change next year, and the year after that? How do we prepare for the pace of change without feeling fatigue? How can we build our capacity for change so we can respond better to market forces?*

Whether fatigue is perceived or real, three approaches can help:

1 | Slow down the pace of change where possible

2 | Build a focus on change resilience or change fitness

3 | Provide good change management.

1. SLOW DOWN THE PACE OF CHANGE

For an organisation to remain competitive, it must be responsive to change. The challenge for organisations looking to slow down the pace of change is that change now is constant and relentless. Organisations must easily adapt to market forces in the external business environment, such as regulatory changes, industry trends, customer expectations, economic demands, competitor activity, and numerous other political and social forces.

It may be difficult to slow down the pace of change when market forces dictate otherwise. An organisation with a higher level of change maturity is likely to be more capable or *fit* to take on a greater volume of change. A business cannot afford to say, 'We need a rest from change this year because we are *change fatigued*.' For many organisations, it may be unrealistic to expect to stay in business, yet ask for a change sabbatical!

2. BUILD A FOCUS ON CHANGE RESILIENCE

We are more change resilient than we think. Think about the change you've absorbed in the last few years. It will be change in the way you consume information and read news, the way you listen to music, how you book travel, order food, learn, order taxis, watch movies and programs, do your shopping, find directions to reach a destination by car, meet other people, play games, access user manuals, monitor your fitness, and of course, how you communicate with others.

I run an activity with workshop participants to gather ideas - one post-it note per idea - on things we are using or doing in our professional and personal lives that we weren't using 15 years ago, and that we can't imagine not being in our lives now. After completing the activity, we realise how much we have adopted with little or no resistance, and this reminds us how adaptive we really are. In an article I wrote on LinkedIn, I called this *adoption creep.*

There are three key lessons from this activity:

Lesson 1: We underestimate our capacity for change

One comment from a participant really packed a punch with the group: *Wow, we really underrate our own change fitness, don't we?*

An awareness of the volume and scope of *adoption creep* gives us confidence that, given the right circumstances, we are extremely adaptive and resilient. With that confidence in our capacity, we can explore what creates those conditions for receptiveness, and then how we can create the same conditions for change in organisations.

Lesson 2: It springboards co-creation

Asking employees how they have responded to incremental change in the past, helps them understand how and why they adopt change easily. This opens a conversation about what will help them adopt workplace change and how they can co-create a positive experience.

The activity engages people in exploring what success looks like, giving them a positive view of the new world. The key benefit for change practitioners is that we gain insights into how a desired future state looks from a user's perspective. And it prompts the question: *How can we help you adopt change more easily at work? It's happening all the time - we can do this together.* This approach legitimises a discussion about what our people think and how they feel, and then can anchor it to the positive adoption narrative that is taking place largely in their personal lives.

Lesson 3: It helps us reframe our language

As mentioned in the last chapter, the language we use when we talk about change can make a big difference.

The *adoption creep* activity reminds us that fatigue may not be a common response to change. If we revisit the notion that change brings a range of responses, including positive outcomes, it helps us plan for deep engagement through co-creation and collaboration. In the conversations it opens, we can 'unpack' emotional responses and why people feel fatigued.

Interestingly, the words *resistance* and *fatigue* rarely crop up in this activity. The focus is on positive language such as *change fitness, resilience, adaptive* and *response.*

When we consider the amount of change we've absorbed in the last few decades, it begs the question about how real change fatigue is at an individual level.

3. PROVIDE GOOD CHANGE MANAGEMENT

We know that organisations and leaders need to become more adaptive and build change resilience into their DNA. But what can we do, as change practitioners, when the 'fatigue' word crops up despite our best efforts to reframe the language and focus on change resilience?

Dr Jen Frahm explores this very situation, with some tips in her article on the sentiment of fatigue:

- Introduce change with context. Explain the *why* and the *what's in it for me*, particularly as part of a bigger change program underway.
- Leverage the benefits of the retrospective. You could consider the retrospective as a ritual to mark endings, note lessons learned and welcome new beginnings. This re-energises a team

with optimism and purpose. The retrospective is explained in the chapter *Agile change activity*.

REFRAME THE LANGUAGE

I also recommend avoiding the term 'change fatigue' in your change readiness surveys. I've seen surveys in organisations that are titled *Change Fatigue Scale*. Because language and words are powerful primers of our thoughts, such an approach may draw attention to a negative emotion. *The word 'fatigue' itself is already priming us for a state of being tired.*

NUDGE THE MINDSET

To help nudge the mindset into being more adaptive, look for opportunities to replace the term *change fatigue* with *change fitness* or *change resilience*.

We can talk about 'change' as continuous improvement, and be comfortable discussing what doesn't work, and talking about our failures as learning opportunities. Creating a climate where it's safe to experiment and fail in the workplace helps lift morale and build change fitness.

The mindset needed for a climate of continuous change is not about: *Can we really afford to implement this change?* Rather, it's about: *Can we afford NOT to change?*

REDUCE THE THREAT RESPONSE

Good change leadership and management practices help reduce the sentiment of change fatigue.

Create opportunity for engagement with co-creation. Look for ways to involve your end users early to reduce uncertainty and promote a sense of autonomy. From the research carried out by David Rock and his SCARF model, we know that addressing uncertainty and autonomy will reduce the threat response. By offering anchors of certainty and choices where we can, we are providing proven antidotes for feeling worn out and disengaged.

It's insightful to ask your stakeholders and end users to do a 'stock take' of the volume of change we've absorbed, as individuals, in both our personal and professional lives in less than one generation. This process helps them appreciate our innate capacity for change resilience and *adoption creep.*

As humans, we respond to change in different ways depending on whether we see the change as positive or negative. As we saw in the last chapter on change resistance, we know some people are excited by change and welcome it when they see a gain or reward associated with it.

💡 GOOD TO KNOW

The reasons for the fatigue or 'perceived fatigue' are numerous and are often rooted in experiences with poorly executed change.

To talk about change fatigue is to assume that everyone experiences the same response to change, which we know is not true.

We all know that change is relentless and continuous – that *new normal* stuff. So when I hear chatter about change fatigue, I question it early and am reminded of this saying:

> *When the winds of change blow,*
> *Some build walls and*
> *Others build windmills.*

The windmills represent change fitness or change resilience.

Dr Jen Frahm and I also explore the topic of change fatigue in one of our #brain-pickers episodes - the links can be found on my website.

RELEVANT CHAPTERS: Enterprise change management, Change resistance, Agile change activity, Brain-friendly change

\#

The reasons for change fatigue or 'perceived fatigue' are numerous and often rooted in experiences with poorly executed change. #changeessentials

23

CHANGE PARABLES

A parable is an effective way to communicate a message or principles that will resonate, will be remembered, and can easily be re-told. For this reason, leadership development programs often feature parables as part of the learning, to open team discussions and to provoke thinking.

Let's take a closer look at four parables that are commonly applied to change management.

1. THE TWO SIDES OF CHANGE: CRISIS OR OPPORTUNITY?

While the exact origins of this ancient story remain unknown, it is believed to be Taoist. This tale of a wise farmer from a poor Chinese village illustrates the dual aspects of change.

- *One day the farmer's horse runs away, leaving him without his reliable animal to help him work the land. His neighbour comes to offer sympathy, saying, 'Too bad about your horse.' The farmer simply replies, 'Maybe.'*
- *The next day the farmer's horse comes back leading two wild horses into the stable. This time the neighbour congratulates the farmer, saying, 'What a lucky break!' Again the farmer replies, 'Maybe.'*
- *The next day the farmer's son breaks his leg trying to tame one of the wild horses, and again the neighbour comes over to offer sympathy.*

'Too bad,' says the neighbour. Once again the farmer simply replies, 'Maybe.'

- *The next day the recruitment officer from the emperor's army comes through the region taking all the young men of fighting age, but since the farmer's son has a broken leg he is left behind. The story can go on and on.*

This story explains how change will be perceived differently by various people, and how perceptions can change over time. We never really know how the farmer was feeling as he offered little comment or response, despite provocation from his neighbour.

It also sends a message that 'things happen for the best'.

2. THE MONKEYS IN THE CAGE

This parable is rumoured to have started as an experiment in the 1960s. It explains how old behaviours can continue to shape organisational culture. It goes like this:

- *There are five monkeys in a cage. Beyond their reach, high up, is a bunch of bananas. Just underneath the bananas is a ladder. One monkey climbs the ladder and is sprayed with cold water, along with the four other monkeys watching. All five monkeys sit on the floor, cold and still hungry.*
- *So another monkey attempts the climb up the ladder. Again, they are all sprayed with cold water. A third monkey starts the climb but the other monkeys pull him down as they know the 'consequences'.*
- *One monkey is removed and replaced with a new starter. As he eyes off the bananas, he quickly goes for the ladder but the other monkeys drag him down. One by one, the original monkeys are replaced by newbies. Each time one tries to climb the ladder, they are pulled away and back down, even though not one of the monkeys in this new group has ever been sprayed with cold water.*

Whether the 'experiment' really took place or not, is of little relevance. How often have you started working at a place and you question a practice, only to be told 'that's just how we do things around here'? Is it because there was once a punitive culture, or 'unwritten rules', that no one wants to challenge? It reminds us to question habits, rituals and practices that may be out-of-date, or serve an 'old master'.

Parables as books

The next two parables are well-known books that have made their mark in change management:

- *Who Moved My Cheese?*
- *Our Iceberg Is Melting.*

3. WHO MOVED MY CHEESE?

Who Moved My Cheese? was written in 1998 by Spencer Johnson, the co-author of another popular leadership book in the 1980s, *The One Minute Manager*. Like many fables, this parable has key characters, each with names, who set out on a quest.

Even though the book is now over 20 years old, it is still often referred to, typically to help people understand different responses to change; and it promotes awareness of our own responses, as we can identify with the qualities and attributes of each of the four main characters.

- *Four characters live in a maze: two mice, Scurry and Sniff, and two little people, Hem and Haw. Nearby is a wonderful supply of their favourite food - cheese (of course!). Hem and Haw have moved their homes to be near the food. Meanwhile, Scurry and Sniff have always run around the maze corridors and corners looking for their cheese.*
- *One day (yes, because one day something always changes) the cheese is gone! Somehow they didn't notice that their supply was diminishing. When Scurry and Sniff saw the early signs of cheese*

> *supply decreasing, they quickly changed tack and started looking elsewhere... successfully.*

- *On the other hand, Hem and Haw felt a sense of injustice. Instead of looking for new cheese, they kept returning to the place of their original supply in hope it would simply reappear.*

This story contrasts resilience to resistance - a closed or fixed mindset to an open, learning mindset. It sends a powerful message about the benefits of adopting a positive response to change. Nothing stays the same and we need to build resilience to adapt quickly. The more quickly you can let go of 'old cheese', the more quickly you will find 'new cheese'!

4. OUR ICEBERG IS MELTING

Co-authored in 2006 by John Kotter and Holger Rathgeber, this book is about changing and succeeding in any conditions, following John Kotter's eight-step change process. There are numerous analogies with workplace change, including change champions, executive leadership teams, influence and resistance.

This time our characters are based in a penguin colony:

- *Fred is the curious and observant colony member (penguin) who senses danger when he notices that the iceberg they live on is starting to melt. In this colony we have a Leadership Council of 10 members headed by Alice, who is approachable but no push-over.*
- *The story continues with the engagement between Fred and the Leadership Council, and explains how this imposed change is handled by various personalities who express fear, denial, resistance, different leadership styles and responses, along with typical office politics.*

A key message here, as succinctly described by John Kotter himself is: *Handle the challenge of change well, and you can prosper greatly. Handle it poorly, and you put yourself and others at risk.*

GOOD TO KNOW

Parables are effective ways to introduce sessions and open discussions about change, and to uncover how people are feeling. By exploring response through fictional stories, you can create a safe environment for people to talk, or nudge them to reflect on their reactions and behaviours.

RELATED CHAPTERS: Change communication

#

Parables are effective ways to introduce sessions and open discussions about change, and to uncover how people are feeling. By exploring response through fictional stories, you can create a safe environment for people to talk, or nudge them to reflect on their reactions and behaviours. #changeessentials

24

PROJECT
MANAGEMENT AND
CHANGE MANAGEMENT

As most change initiatives are delivered as part of a project, there is an expectation that change practitioners have an understanding of project management principles, methodologies and responsibilities.

Project management capability for a change manager can be defined as:

Understands and applies project management principles to change planning and delivery, including project planning, risk management, project process adherence, relevant project tools, reporting and governance, to ensure that the change activity is delivered effectively.

Just like project sponsors and change practitioners, not all project or program managers are created equal. Depending on their previous exposure to change management as a dedicated discipline, their expectations and understanding of the change practitioner's role varies greatly.

Some people may think that project management and change management are the same thing. Clarifying the difference provides an opportunity for the change professional to help project team members understand and value their role and capabilities.

WHAT'S THE DIFFERENCE?

While they work closely together on the same project at the same time, project management and change management are very different disciplines.

Project management is focused on the *implementation* of a product or a service. The discipline applies a structured approach to deliver the project objectives with planned tasks and deliverables. Project management monitors the quality of the work through a triangle model also referred to as the *Triple Constraint* of *scope, cost* and *time*.

Change management, by contrast, is focused on the people side of the change initiative, particularly *buy-in* and *adoption*. I often use the diagram below to show the key roles for each discipline, and to highlight that change management is primarily about people and performance:

PROJECTS AND CHANGE

PROJECT MANAGEMENT
IMPLEMENTATION

A structured approach to effect change that identifies scope, tasks, activities and deliverables to achieve project objectives.

BENEFITS

BUDGETS

RISKS & ISSUES

SCOPE

TIME

SYSTEMS & WORKFLOW

PROJECT TEAM

CHANGE MANAGEMENT
ADOPTION

A structured approach that empowers people to change behaviours and equips them with tools and processes to succeed in the new state.

BEHAVIOUR CHANGE

CULTURE CHANGE

HUMAN RESPONSE

READINESS FROM DAY 1

WITH SKILLS, KNOWLEDGE & MINDSET

PERFORMANCE SUPPORT

Although the two disciplines are complementary, they don't always operate in the same way across, and even within, organisations. There are three ways in which change management and project management may work together:

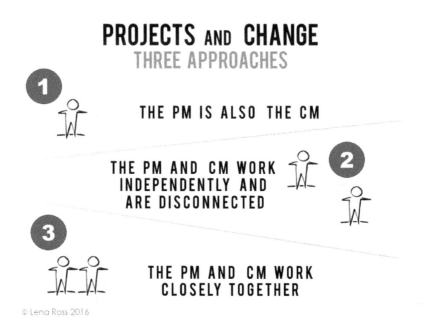

PROJECTS AND CHANGE
THREE APPROACHES

1 THE PM IS ALSO THE CM

THE PM AND CM WORK
INDEPENDENTLY AND
ARE DISCONNECTED 2

3 THE PM AND CM WORK
CLOSELY TOGETHER

© Lena Ross 2016

Approach 1: The Project Manager is also the Change Manager

- In some way or another, the project manager is juggling both responsibilities, typically on a smaller project or a Business as Usual change initiative.
- This may occur in a larger organisation, where change managers are employed, but on a small change initiative one person is assigned to carry out the two roles.
- In this scenario, the change practitioner in unlikely to have any influence as we are often not even made aware of the scenario, or invited to support the initiative.
- If we are aware of this situation, we can play a role in providing the project manager with some guidance and simple change management templates to help them with activities such as identifying impacts, communications planning and preparing a change plan on a page.

💡 GOOD TO KNOW

A person who carries out the dual role of both project manager and change manager may be referred to as a *slashie* because of the slash in their title, eg project/change manager. *Slashie* is a term used for someone who carries out more than one role or function.

Approach 2: The Project Manager and the Change Manager are working on the same project but operate rather independently

- This appears to be a disconnect, with little overlap in, or discussion about, their work; in this situation, the two managers are working separately due to little or no engagement or consultation.
- In this non-ideal situation, the project manager is unlikely to appreciate the value of change management or fully understand the rationale behind change activity.
- To address the apparent separation, the change consultant can take steps towards building a more consolidated plan that considers an integrated approach.

Approach 3: The Project Manager and the Change Manager work closely together

- This is an integrated approach, where the two managers have great respect for each other's roles and responsibilities, and a mutual understanding of how the two disciplines support each other.
- It provides a framework for clarity on responsibilities and which activities are carried out together. Clearly, this is the ideal way to work together.

A FRAMEWORK TO DRIVE DISCUSSION

An aligned roadmap is a great way to open discussions with your project manager. It will provide role clarity and help you agree on key activity and areas of joint accountability. This is an example only and does not represent all the activities and responsibilities of project management and change management:

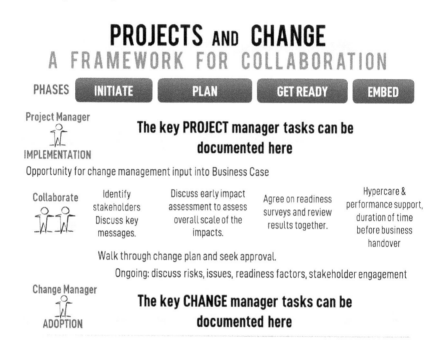

THE BUSINESS CASE FOR INTEGRATION

Integration ensures alignment of the technical, business, behavioural and mindset changes required of people, to achieve the project's business benefits.

The business case for integrating the two disciplines is compelling if we look at the *Prosci Best Practices in Change Management Benchmarking Report 2018*. The report's results reveal that 75% of the survey participants took an integrated approach to change management and project management. The research showed that when the two disciplines were integrated, there was a higher rate of project success. It revealed that 50%

of participants who did integrate were able to meet or exceed their project objectives, compared to 35% of those who did not integrate.

💡 GOOD TO KNOW

A note on interpretation of the word 'change':

Be mindful of the context of the word 'change' AND how it's used in your project. On system implementation projects, requests are made and documented for system changes.

In project language, a *change request* is a formal and documented process that details an alteration to what was previously agreed, for a product or system.

The term *change request* is often misunderstood, as it's described as part of the 'change management' process in project literature. However, this is not a change management capability or responsibility. The main thing to note is that this is neither a people-related change nor the responsibility of the change consultant.

Because a *change request* has the potential to reshape the scope of the project deliverables, it may impact project timelines and proposed change activities.

Typically, the project manager (or a delegate such as the project analyst) manages the process. The change requests are documented in a 'change request form', logged, and discussed at team meetings to assess the impact on the project in terms of budget, scope and schedule. The request needs to be approved by the designated approver, who is usually the project sponsor.

You may also hear reference to *change control, change registers, change logs, change advisory boards,* or *change control boards.* Ask for clarification when you are not sure what a term means in the context of your project. For example, the term *change control* is typically the process of managing changes made to a product or system. Most of these are outside the scope of organisational change management.

MORE GOOD TO KNOW

The RACI matrix

Something you will come across, and may need to complete as a change practitioner, is a RACI matrix, also known as a Responsibility Assignment Matrix (RAM). RACI is an acronym for *Responsible, Accountable, Consult* and *Inform*. The purpose of this document is to clearly define project roles and responsibilities. Presented in an easy-to-read table format, it's a quick reference guide that shows who does what, who needs to know and who needs to be consulted, by activity, decision or milestone.

RACI definitions:

RACI item	Definition
R – Responsible *The doer*	The doer is the individual(s) who actually completes the task end-to-end. The doer is responsible for action and implementation. Responsibility can be shared. The degree of responsibility is determined by the individual with 'A'.
A – Accountable *The buck stops here, they are on the hook*	The accountable person is the individual who is ultimately answerable for the activity or decision. This includes 'yes' or 'no' authority and veto power. Note: Only one 'A' can be assigned.
C – Consult *In the loop, provide input*	The consult role is the individual(s) who is typically a subject matter expert, who is consulted *prior* to a final decision or action. This is a pre-determined need for *two-way* communication. Input from this designated position is required.
I – Inform *Keep in the picture, copied in, FYI*	The individual(s) who needs to be informed *after* a decision or action is taken. They may be required to take action as a result of the outcome. It's a *one-way* communication.

THE DIFFERENCE BETWEEN A PROJECT AND A PROGRAM

Like many terms in change management and project management, specific definitions and characteristics may vary across organisations.

It is broadly accepted that the difference between a program and project is that a *program*, or *program of work* is a collection of projects. A program is likely to employ a *change lead*, who oversees the work of change consultants who work on each project within that program of work.

CONTRIBUTION TO PROJECT STATUS REPORTS

As change practitioners, we are asked (in almost all projects if not all) to contribute to the Project Status Report, which forms part of project compliance and governance requirements.

This presents a brilliant opportunity to showcase the change activity taking place and what it's achieved, and to create a *change dashboard* for consistent and visual reporting, particularly on the change success measures. If you are asked to complete a RAG table, this stands for Red, Amber and Green and is also known as *traffic light reporting* on the status of your deliverables.

PROJECT RISKS AND ISSUES

Risk and issues are raised and documented in a *Risk Register* to identify what may prevent the project's quality and progress, and what can be done to minimise, remove or address them. Risk and issues impact the *Triple Constraint* (mentioned at the beginning of this chapter) of time, cost and/or scope.

It's helpful to know the difference between a risk and an issue. This diagram is the most useful one I've found to explain the difference: a *risk* is something that has not yet happened, but will possibly occur; an *issue* is an event that has already taken place.

PROJECTS AND CHANGE
RISK VS ISSUE

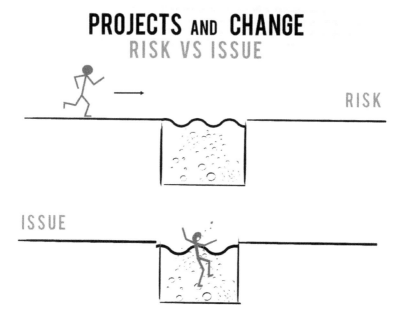

💡 GOOD TO KNOW

If you hear reference to the PMBOK, this is the abbreviation for the Project Management Body of Knowledge. This resource details guidelines and terminology for project management. Originally published in 1996 and regularly updated, it is widely accepted as the key resource (or bible) for project and program management.

There is a great deal of information on project management for the curious among you who want to learn more. As they are complementary disciplines, it's not unusual for change consultants to switch to project management, and sometimes we see the reverse - project management professionals becoming change practitioners.

RELATED CHAPTERS: Change sponsorship, Change capabilities, Change planning

AGILE CHANGE MANAGEMENT

25

GETTING ON THE SAME
PAGE WITH AGILE

For a long time, where linear, waterfall-style projects were mainstream, change was delivered in a linear approach with a list of artefacts to complete. Now, in a climate of complex and continuous change, there is an increasing expectation that change programs will be leaner and deliver outcomes in shorter cycles. This means change practitioners will encounter agile as a way of doing and being in their work.

Entire books, in the thousands, have been written about agile with various perspectives. For the change practitioner to understand what it means, it's best to explore agile in the context of the Agile Manifesto, agile in software development and projects, agile as an organisational or business capability, and the principles to apply when delivering change.

This chapter is designed to provide an introduction to the uninitiated, and to explain the difference between the software development context and the broader application of the word *agile*. It's almost identical to the chapter with the same title in my first book *Hacking for Agile Change,* so if you've already read that, feel free to skip to the next chapter, or speed read ahead!

BIG A, LITTLE A

You may find yourself chatting to a colleague and the 'a' word crops up in conversation. Then your agile-savvy colleague asks you: 'Oh, do you mean agile with a big A or agile with a little a?'

I've discovered that the two versions of the word *agile* - capitalised and all lower case - are often used interchangeably. A common understanding is helpful, so you can be on the same page as your stakeholders. This is how I start the conversation: I draw the following diagram on a sheet of paper in my notebook. I deliberately draw it at the time, rather than bring a printed version, so it invites input.

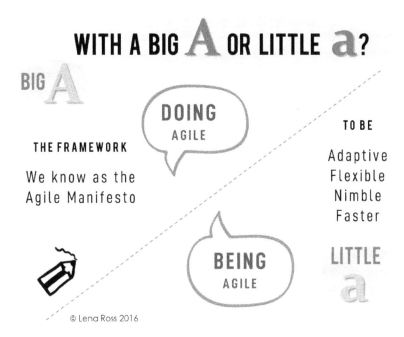

In my workshops, I prepare the same diagram on flipchart paper. There is white space to invite participants to add their thoughts and definitions throughout the session.

I explain that it's common practice in the Agile community to use the *big A* when referring to the Agile Manifesto and its associated practices. This is often referred to as *doing* agile. The *little a* is the adjective we use to describe something adaptive, flexible, nimble, quicker of mind and faster in movement. An athlete is nimble in action, just as an insightful thinker is agile of mind. By contrast, this is referred to as *being* agile.

I've used the following description to help illustrate the difference:

··

When an organisation wants to become more agile, they look for ways to: be responsive to external forces, be adaptive, deliver services and products to customers faster, think outside the box, and eliminate waste to improve effectiveness. To help them achieve this, they recruit coaches and project managers with experience in Agile software and product development.

··

 GOOD TO KNOW

Projects using Agile practices alone will not make the organisation agile, as this also requires people to adopt and model the right mindset and behaviours. Agile (yes, big A) project approaches will help, but will not achieve this alone. That's *little a* agile - what the word meant, and still does, before the *Agile Manifesto* was created. The goal here is that you don't hold off including change practices in your change plan just because you are not working on an official Agile project.

THE HISTORY OF BIG A

To provide some clarity on Agile (yes, with a *big A*), let's take a brief look at where it started. If you've been reading or talking about Agile/agile, no doubt you've heard of the Agile Manifesto.

The Agile Manifesto, designed for software development, was written back in 2001. Its intent was not to be anti-methodology, but to bring about a balanced view that would welcome adjustments and pace. In the Manifesto we can see the elements that are core to change practitioners in an agile world: a focus on the customer, a nimble approach and value placed on people over process.

The Agile Manifesto is made up of:
- Four values
- 12 principles.

AGILE VALUES

The values mantra states that: *While there is value in the items on the right, we value the items on the left more.*

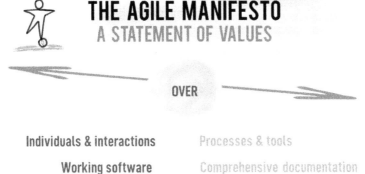

THE AGILE MANIFESTO
A STATEMENT OF VALUES

OVER

Individuals & interactions	Processes & tools
Working software	Comprehensive documentation
Customer collaboration	Contract negotiation
Responding to change	Following a plan

SOURCE: www.agilemanifesto.org

AGILE PRINCIPLES

The Agile Manifesto's 12 principles state:
- Our highest priority is to satisfy the customer through early and continuous delivery of valuable software.
- We welcome changing requirements, even late in development. Agile processes harness change for the customer's competitive advantage.

- We will deliver working software frequently, from a couple of weeks to a couple of months, with a preference for the shorter timescale.
- Business people and developers must work together daily throughout the project.
- We will build projects around motivated individuals, give them the environment and support they need, and trust them to get the job done.
- The most efficient and effective method of conveying information to and within a development team is face-to-face conversation.
- Working software is the primary measure of progress.
- Agile processes promote sustainable development. The sponsors, developers, and users should be able to maintain a constant pace indefinitely.
- Continuous attention to technical excellence and good design enhances agility.
- Simplicity - the art of maximising the amount of work not done - is essential.
- The best architectures, requirements, and designs emerge from self-organising teams.
- At regular intervals, the team reflects on how to become more effective, then tunes and adjusts its behaviour accordingly.

Source: www.agilemanifesto.org

While the values and principles are software-centric, the application can be extended to non-software projects, especially with the themes of lean, team behaviours and customer-centricity.

We can see how the principles and value of *big A* also apply to *little a*. But *little a* is agile about everything, with an application that is broader, particularly in reference to an organisation being agile.

BUSTING MYTHS ABOUT AGILE

The definitions of *big A* and *little a* can cause confusion. This makes it easy for Agile/agile sceptics to jump to conclusions that have given Agile/agile some bad press. You'll hear or read about myths, most of which are not true. Some make Agile/agile sound like complete anarchy. Here are some common myths to explode right now:

Myth 1: Agile is just Scrum

Reality: Scrum is a framework for developing and managing work. *Agile* is an umbrella word for practices such as Scrum, so Scrum is one of many practices belonging to Agile. Agile is so much more!

Myth 2: Agile means no plan

Reality: Planning is different, not absent. Up-front planning is replaced with more iterative, adaptive process. This means you will see numerous revised plans, not just one plan. There are more plans developed at a greater frequency due to the iterative nature of regular review. The Agile Manifesto's 12 principles ensure that Agile is not anarchy.

Myth 3: Agile means no project managers

Reality: Agile management definitely needs project managers. They are often called Scrum Masters. Team roles are different, demanding a different type of leadership and team dynamic, and ultimately how work gets done.

Myth 4: Agile means no documentation

Reality: This may be wishful thinking for some, but documentation has a place in Agile. There are design documents that add value by providing information on the Minimum Viable Product (MVP). Documentation is iterative with records of all previous versions and documents that drive (not replace) conversations with stakeholders. MVP refers to an artefact with enough features or information to demonstrate or provide a solution. If you come across teams who say they don't need documentation because they are agile, it's the time to remind them that the four values of the Agile Manifesto don't dismiss documentation - the statement is designed to emphasise value on working software *over* comprehensive documentation, not *instead* of it.

Myth 5: Agile only works for developers

Reality: Whilst Agile started with a focus on software development, it's now been applied more broadly. Any project type can use Agile approaches to improve delivery.

Myth 6: Agile is the silver bullet

Reality: Find me a silver bullet and we will all be out of jobs! Agile is not the panacea for all our organisational challenges. It needs the right leadership, behaviours and mindset to support it. Agile practices alone will not make your business nimble and adaptive.

AGILE AS AN ORGANISATIONAL CAPABILITY

Agility is so much more than a software development approach or a project methodology. It's a mindset, along with a set of behaviours and practices. As business leaders are making sense of agile and looking to build business or enterprise agility, defining agile as a capability demystifies the word itself, and helps us understand what it means for individuals, teams and organisations.

To explain this, I've developed this pyramid model that shows the layers of agile as a capability. The fourth layer, at the base, is *organisational agility*. For an organisation to become agile, it needs people with capability in each of these three parts: people who are agile in their thinking, their actions and in their practices.

AGILE AS A CAPABILITY

What you **DO & DELIVER**

How you **ACT**

How you **THINK**

PRACTICES

BEHAVIOURS

MINDSET

ORGANISATIONAL AGILITY

© Lena Ross 2016

1. *Agile mindset - how you THINK*

    Being truly agile in what you do and deliver, starts with an agility in mindset. It's this mindset that is open to learning and trying new things, is comfortable with uncertainty, is intensely curious, dares to experiment and is not frightened to fail.

2. *Agile behaviours - how you ACT*

    Agile behaviours at a team, and individual, level can be broadly described as behaviours that rely on collaboration, transparency, honesty, willingness to work outside their area of expertise, adaptability, and openness to feedback so they can continuously improve their practices.

3. *Agile practice - what you DO and DELIVER*

    There are numerous agile practices that work best when the team members demonstrate agile behaviours and mindset. Of course, you don't need to be working on a project that's officially declared 'agile' to apply agile practices, such as stand-up meetings and Kanban boards.

Simply put, to be agile is a *mindset* AND a *skill set*. For change managers AND change leaders, this means we're delivering change in an environment that's demanding faster and more people-centred outcomes.

In the following chapters we will explore what this means for agile change delivery.

RELATED CHAPTERS: Agile change delivery, Agile change activity

Projects using Agile ceremonies and practices alone will not make the organisation agile. Enterprise or business agility requires all people, including leaders, to adopt and model the right mindset and behaviours. #changeessentials

26

AGILE CHANGE
DELIVERY

Some questions that have been circulating in the change industry for some time are:

So we have agile, we have hybrid projects that are managed as a mix of agile and waterfall, and we have waterfall - now what?

What do I need to do as a change practitioner?

What exactly is 'agile change management'?

Is there an agile change management process or a framework for me to follow? And how do we deliver it?

SO WHAT IS AGILE CHANGE MANAGEMENT?

I define agile change management as a *practice that draws on the ethos of the Agile Manifesto, to adaptively deliver the right solution at the right time.*

Based on this, we can define this approach as *agile change delivery,* or *adaptive change delivery.*

Agile change delivery is about planning and delivering change with a reduced reliance on step-by-step processes, which often result in artefacts we may not need. It's about drawing on the principles of lean, agile, brain science and design thinking, and shifting our mindset from following one change framework to a more adaptive approach. It's a shift from being process-centric to principles-based.

 GOOD TO KNOW

If you want to maintain a sequencing approach to change activity, you can continue to use the familiar project activity clusters, such as *design, engage, plan, iterate, implement* and *reflect* – but with an adaptive approach, rather than planning and delivering change in the same way for all change initiatives.

GUIDING PRINCIPLES

So, as a change practitioner, how can you deliver agile change in your organisation? Here are five guiding principles to keep in mind:

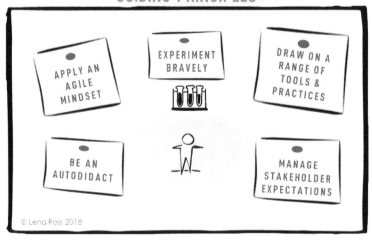

1. *Apply an agile mindset*

To be adaptive in your delivery means you can respond to changing requirements and adjust your change plans. I've seen many change managers express disappointment or frustration over the need to recast their plans to adjust to shifting priorities.

The last chapter introduced a brief definition of the agile mindset as one that demonstrates openness to learning and new ideas, along with comfort with uncertainty. Adaptive delivery requires this nimble mindset to embrace ambiguity and experiment with a natural curiosity. For a change practitioner, this also means *an ability to be adaptive to the needs of the change initiative, while integrating agile practices in change planning and delivery.*

This mindset helps you let go of the need for perfection, especially if you are attached to the need to develop a perfect document before you circulate it. I have a passion for infographics and material with high visual impact. It took me a (long) while to learn that I was spending a wee bit too much time perfecting my visuals. I learned that having a meeting with a stakeholder with an 'imperfect' artefact is okay.

Manage expectations and explain that your document is in draft, and you are covering points for *discussion and iteration.* Drawing on a whiteboard or flip chart paper was a way of discussing the change that promoted a good deal more co-creation and engagement than rocking up to a meeting with a big, colourful PowerPoint slide deck. The very fact that a document doesn't have a high gloss finish is what invites collaboration. When I saw the value of taking this approach, it shifted my thinking to 'adaptive delivery'.

This is also consistent with the Agile Manifesto value of *individuals and interactions over processes and tools.*

As a change manager, you can play a role in influencing others by:

- Modelling an agile mindset to help your team and peers get on board.
- Being curious, and asking questions as if you are a start-up. A beginner's mindset doesn't judge; it puts aside previous learnings and experiences and listens objectively with deep empathy.

The agile mindset equips us with resilience so we can recognise failures as opportunities to learn rather than personal setbacks, and it enables us to work more effectively in an increasingly complex and ambiguous environment.

2. *Experiment bravely*

To think like a start-up is to accept a healthy dose of risk, to experiment, and to learn quickly from failure along the way. Shifting our perception of failure isn't too easy, especially because 'failure' has had bad press together with a long association with negativity.

Angela Duckworth, author of *Grit: The Power of Passion and Perseverance,* suggests looking for opportunities to fail as a way to build a tolerance for failure, labelling it 'exposure therapy'. One suggestion is that if you are a writer, send your manuscript to so many publishers that rejection notices will outnumber positive responses. Find ways to experience rejection to build resilience.

It's not just our schooling that has associated failure with punishment. Through our working lives, successful outcomes and solutions are typically rewarded and celebrated over experimenting and learning from mistakes. We have not been well conditioned for 'grit' to test, fail and learn.

Change can't happen if you are deterred by the fear of failure. Reframe your view of failure to one of experiment.

You can start by experimenting *safely* with practices such as working out loud, using visual management tools such as Kanban boards, enterprise social networks and stand-up meetings. Whether or not your project is officially declared as agile, at the end of each implementation, there's no reason why you can't introduce agile practices - such as a retrospective - to capture lessons for future improvement.

As humans, we're hardwired to mimic others, so simply modelling behaviours and practices will rub off!

3.   *Draw on a range of tools and practices*

Keep in mind that there isn't one prescribed way or process to successfully deliver change. This may be a surprise, or even disappointing to some, especially if you're used to following step-by-step change frameworks. Think of agile as a way of *thinking* and *doing* where you have access to a broad range of practices and tools you can choose from, depending on your change initiative.

It's not as complex as it may sound. To explain the 'principles not formula' approach in my workshops, I use the metaphor of the sushi train. A sushi train is the Australasian restaurant adaptation of the Japanese *Kaiten-zushi*, where the food options appear on a conveyer belt that can be accessed by the customers. You can pick the food you want, when you want. In your toolkit, you have knowledge and expertise in hundreds of change models, interventions, advice and activities. Think of all the tools, practices, templates and information you have at your disposal, and imagine them sitting on a revolving sushi train. They are there for you to pick when you need them - to 'right-size' your change approach. If you don't need it for today's change initiative, it will always be there, on the train, ready for you to pick up if you need it on your next assignment.

4.   *Be an autodidact*

As information evolves so quickly, we know that books and blogs alone will not provide all the answers. This means that we will learn fast, we'll make mistakes, we'll learn as we go, from each other and by connecting, to keep our knowledge and skills relevant.

If you're not already a lifelong learner, now is the time to jump on board. Learning is less likely to be provided for you, in the traditional face-to-face forum, in the VUCA environment (volatility, uncertainty, complexity and ambiguity). Lifelong self-directed learning is a necessity, not only to stay abreast of what's happening, but also to achieve mastery in your chosen field.

Curiosity is a critical element in developing and maintaining an agile mindset. Don't wait for scheduled learning events. If you want to future-proof your value either as an employee or independent consultant, self-directed learning is critical. It's likely a great deal of that learning will be through informal channels. There is even a word for a person who is self-taught, outside the typical classroom or educational channels - it's an *autodidact*. Cool word, hey?

5.   *Manage stakeholder expectations*

Whether it's software implementation or not, we need to consider what is right for the customer and end user and how we can do it most efficiently, and we need to be adaptive in the way we plan and deliver change in an agile way.

I often refer to right-sizing the change effort as *Goldilocks change management.* In the familiar fairy tale of the three bears, Goldilocks has three options - one that is too much, one that is too little and one that is just right. As in this parable, there's a case for applying the Goldilocks principle of 'just right' in how we deliver change.

When you take a lean approach, sometimes known as Minimum Viable Product (MVP), it needs to be communicated effectively to your stakeholders to manage their expectations. Minimum Viable Product (MVP), a commonly used term in project and change parlance, means delivering a product or artefact with just enough features or information to achieve your objectives or kick off your conversation. But MVP doesn't mean inferior quality, or that we totally discard our entire change management toolkit. It means the change practitioner needs to be adaptive and aware of when to scale up or down.

It's about creating a plan and deliverables that are lighter and *just right* for your change initiative and business. This means we adjust the change efforts to suit the organisation and the scale of the change itself, for all projects – both agile and non-agile.

The nature of right-sizing in itself means there's no prescription for how to be like Goldilocks. The scope and scale of the change initiative itself helps you size your work. The variables are countless and the possibilities are endless. Experience and confidence help, of course, as does an agile mindset.

💡 GOOD TO KNOW

The pressure is on the change practitioner to be increasingly adaptive in their approach. What worked on a project in the bank three years ago is unlikely to hit the mark as an approach on a project in health care today.

These are exciting times to be in change management! Change is now continuous and the new normal, so it's important to stay ahead of industry trends and set up a supportive and safe environment that encourages our peers and stakeholders to try new and different approaches. We need a range of tools and practices, not just the agile ones, for the disruptive and diverse challenges ahead.

There is a short clip produced by FLIMP Studios that summarises these five guiding principles, and you can find it in the Resources section of my website.

In a later chapter, we look at agile practices you can integrate into your change activities.

RELATED CHAPTERS: Getting on the same page with agile, Agile change activity

Agile change management is a practice that draws on the ethos of the Agile Manifesto, to adaptively deliver the right solution at the right time. #changeessentials

Change can't happen if you are deterred by the fear of failure. Reframe your view of failure to one of experiment. #changeessentials

\#

Humans are hardwired to mimic others, so simply modelling behaviours and practices will rub off. #changeessentials

27

PSYCHOLOGICAL
SAFETY

In the last chapter on agile change delivery, one of the five suggested approaches was to 'experiment bravely', and I also mentioned the importance of experimenting 'safely'.

For agile or new ways of working, it is critical that you are in a climate of *psychological safety,* where it's safe to experiment and safe to make mistakes. Think about teams you have worked in. Can you recall a time when you felt it was safe to raise issues, to make suggestions, disclose your mistakes, and even to be a little vulnerable? Were you ever in a place without fear of reprisal, ridicule or punishment? Hopefully, you have experienced all of that. This is what *psychological safety* at work looks like.

The more you hear about agile and new ways of working, with cross-functional and self-organised teams and iteration, the more you will hear about the importance of psychological safety for optimal performance and innovation.

POWER AND FEAR

Some years ago my early exposure to the notion of psychological safety happened when I trained cabin crew at Qantas Domestic (formerly Australian Airlines). In an aircraft, human error can have significant, if not fatal, results. Air safety investigations revealed that in many instances, it was not only human error that caused aircraft accidents, but also the lack of communication between crew members. Following recommendations from the America-based National Transportation Safety Board (NTSB), we were introduced to Crew Resource Management (CRM) training.

CRM focused on communication skills, particularly in the cockpit, with a proposed framework to make it 'safe' for more junior crew members to raise concerns with their more senior colleagues, particularly the Captain. Eventually, this training was extended to cabin crew members, and for the first time, we saw joint safety training of cabin and cockpit crew at the airline training centre that still operates in Melbourne for Qantas domestic airline crew.

This initiative, also endorsed by NASA, was innovative in a military-based chain of command culture with a high 'authority gradient' (also known as the 'cockpit gradient'). The key objective of CRM was to create a work environment where it was safe to respectfully question a decision or raise a concern that could potentially impact passenger and aircraft safety.

NOT SO NEW REALLY

The term 'psychological safety' isn't entirely new. Back in the 1960s, it was flagged by MIT Professors Edgar Shein and Warren Bennis as an essential ingredient for making people feel secure and receptive to change. It was later researched in 1990 by William Kahn, and again in 1993 by Schein. More recently, there's been a revival through the work of Amy Edmondson, along with research carried out at Google.

MORE RECENT FINDINGS

Amy Edmondson, a professor of leadership and management at Harvard Business School, carried out research on medical teams. She quickly discovered that the better performing teams were admitting to mistakes and discussing them openly. She went on to define psycho-logical safety as a 'shared belief that the team is safe for interpersonal risk taking'.

Since then, Google became increasingly curious about what made a perfect team, and in 2012 Project Aristotle was born. Over two years, Google studied 180 of their own teams with hundreds of interviews and through engaging numerous experts. The research uncovered five elements that make up a successful team, and psychological safety was clearly the most important factor. Google reported that team members experiencing high levels of psychological safety were less likely to leave the organisation, were more innovative, and rated as higher performers overall by senior colleagues.

HOW DOES IT LOOK FOR YOU?

If you are already working in an environment of psychological safety - great news, happy days! Think about what is making it safe, and how you can help perpetuate that feeling.

Creating a place of psychological safety should be the norm, not the exception.

As I say over and over, new ways of working mean new ways of everything, including the way we lead others and behave as team members. It makes sense that a perception of threat or fear will impair performance and productivity.

THE POWER OF MODELLING BEHAVIOURS

In the last chapter, on *Agile change delivery*, I mentioned that as humans we are hardwired to mimic others. This is why the way leaders act is so critical. Behaving in one way and expecting your team members to do something different does not make sense. Yet we see examples of this folly so often in our working lives.

> **GOOD TO KNOW**
>
> Whether we are leading others or not, we need to keep in mind that how we act is noticed and has an impact on others - there is a *ripple effect*. This plays a significant role in how safe people feel around others.

THE RIPPLE EFFECT

Subconscious behaviours create a ripple effect when we are around others. Take this familiar scenario: when we are around people who are negative and constantly complaining, we feel tired and drained; you might even call them emotional vampires. The flip side is that when we surround ourselves with positive, upbeat people, we feel energised. It's no wonder that on some days we are more exhausted than we should be, for no other reason than the company we've kept.

When this happens, we are experiencing *emotional contagion*, which is defined as the *transfer of moods*.

DESIGNED TO ALIGN

The reason it's so easy to absorb others' emotions or even mimic behaviour around us, is that we are hardwired to do so. Mirroring and absorbing the emotions of people around us is an evolutionary survival skill, as it was critical to harmonise with our tribe. Mirroring is a psychological term to describe the behaviour of subconsciously imitating the characteristics of those around us. As social creatures, we are naturally designed to align with moods and emotions, so we mirror others at a subconscious level. And this takes place with both negative and positive emotions.

If you want to watch an amusing clip on how easy it is to mimic the behaviour of people around us, take a look at one of Asch's Conformity Experiments, called the elevator experiment. In this experiment, three 'plants' in the group deliberately face the rear of the elevator, and one person enters and faces the door. It's not long before the one facing the front of the elevator mimics the others and faces the rear. This reminds us how easy it is for us to conform. The experiment became popular when it appeared on television in the early 1960s in a programme called *Candid Camera* as the 'face the rear' elevator test. You can find this clip to watch on YouTube.

At an *individual level*, we are always modelling behaviours - consciously and unconsciously - and the people around us will copy us at a subconscious level. The ripple effect and emotional contagion of how we act has a significant impact on what others will do. Don't under-estimate the effects of your own actions. Be mindful that the way you act will have an immediate impact on how your team members and colleagues feel.

If we want to invite divergent thinking, promote curiosity, and help our people thrive in an environment of ambiguity and complexity, they need to feel safe to speak up, experiment, fail and learn. Awareness of emotional contagion helps us understand the scope of impact one person can have on the people around them.

Whether or not we are formal leaders, it's about rethinking the behaviours we model each day. There are small things we can do to support and create a culture where it's safe to bring our best and whole selves to work. Often, it's simply the awareness of what's happening (or not) that prompts observation, reflection and then action.

RELATED CHAPTERS: Making change stick, Agile change delivery

Being in a climate of *psychological safety,* where it's safe to experiment and safe to make mistakes, is critical for agile or new ways of working. #changeessentials

But whether we are leading others or not, we need to keep in mind that how we act is noticed and has an impact on others - there is a *ripple effect.* This plays a significant role in how safe people feel around others. #changeessentials

28

AGILE CHANGE
ACTIVITY

Because the business and project landscape is changing so quickly, change consultants are finding themselves landing on more projects that, if not fully labelled and operating as 'agile', follow agile practices in some way.

Knowledge of agile practices helps you understand the role you can play as a change consultant when you are asked to support an 'agile' project. Even when you are not 'asked', or not assigned to a project that is formally declared to be 'agile', you can introduce these practices to any change initiative, to more deeply engage your stakeholders.

💡 GOOD TO KNOW

Agile practices can be applied in all your change planning and day-to-day engagement with project team members, stakeholders and end users. The practices will promote deeper engagement and co-creation with your stakeholders. The more you apply agile practices, the more you will be able to nudge team members to follow, and to be more collaborative and transparent.

Here are a few practices that you can adopt in most, if not all, change projects:

- Team stand-up meeting
- Change canvas or Change Plan on a Page
- Kanban board

- Show your work with
  - Showcases
  - Think tanks
- Retrospective.

Team stand-up meeting

One of the most visible agile practices is the team stand-up meeting. Treated like a ritual, this is sometimes referred to as a daily scrum meeting. By being short and frequent, these meetings help teams develop the desired behaviours by becoming more productive and transparent in their work. For that reason, this practice alone requires a shift in behaviour and mindset for many.

The best place for the daily stand-up is in front of your visual management board, where the progress of the team's work is visible. It shouldn't take longer than 15 minutes at the start of each work day. Each team member addresses three questions:

- What I did since the last meeting
- What I will do until the next meeting
- What's getting in my way.

THE TEAM STAND UP MEETING
AN EXAMPLE

15 MINUTES EACH MORNING

WHAT I DID YESTERDAY

WHAT I WILL DO TODAY

WHAT IS GETTING IN MY WAY?

It's worth noting that the daily stand-up meeting doesn't replace all other meetings, such as planning meetings or other catch-up sessions between the scrum master or project manager and team members that need to take place.

Change canvas

As mentioned in the earlier chapter on change planning, the one-page change canvas is the visual document that includes the case for the change and provides early insights into the scope of the initiative, helping build rationale for dedicated change management resources.

THE CHANGE CANVAS
AN EXAMPLE

PRODUCT OWNER..		CHANGE LEAD.................................
Change being introduced........................		Date...
Problem (the WHAT)	Solution (the HOW)	Value Proposition (the WHY)
Customers/stakeholders (WHO)		Time & effort needed/change resources
	- COMMUNICATION -	
Existing channels		Key messages – W I F M
Success criteria		Risks & issues (high level)

© Lena Ross 2016

THE KANBAN BOARD

Kanban is the Japanese word for visual signal or card. Inspired by the lean manufacturing practices at Toyota, the Kanban board is an effective, visual way for agile teams (and any other teams) to display what they are doing and where it's at. Combine it with the stand-up meeting and you have a visual tool at hand to discuss the progress of your work.

One of the objectives of Kanban is to bring attention to the volume of work in process, in the *'doing'* column, in order to reduce it. The idea is to move work along the flow, to the *'done'* column.

At a glance, you not only see the progress, but also the scope and scale of work underway. You can make it more meaningful by colour coding post-it notes, or adding *avatars*, for each team member. For the uninitiated, an avatar is a graphic, cartoon-like representation of a real team member. An avatar adds a fun, colourful element to the visual management board too.

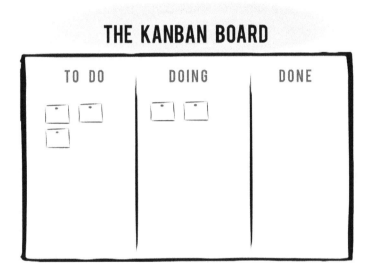

Show your work

Showing your work is similar to *working out loud*, which is explored further in the chapter called *Communicate to co-create,* as one of the four communication channels that promote co-creation and collaboration. Just like working out loud, by showing our work we signal that we are comfortable with it being highly visible to our peers and stakeholders. This practice is consistent with agile team values of transparency and openness about your work. Running a *showcase session* or hosting a *think tank* are two ways to show your work that invite engagement and conversation.

SHOWCASE SESSION

A showcase is a scheduled session or a series of sessions for stakeholders and other employees in your organisation who may be interested in, or impacted by, your change initiative. As the word suggests, it's a great way to 'showcase' your project and the benefits it will deliver.

Schedule your session in a way that invites audience participation. This can be as simple as a quiz, where the answers are provided along the way, with quirky prizes. Or you can keep the energy levels high by breaking up the larger group into smaller groups that rotate to team members who explain or demonstrate a specific part of their work.

Assign your project a hashtag. Keep the interest alive during and after these sessions by asking people to post their key take-aways and photos on your organisation's enterprise social platform. The enterprise social network is the place for questions and answers before, during and after your event. With the hashtag, participants and team members can easily search and find relevant posts.

THINK TANK

I often call my think tanks 'think-ubators' to send a message that thinking is evolving. The think-ubator can be a permanent room or work area where the project team resides, or an assigned area close to the project team.

The think-ubator, or think tank, is a highly visual, often colourful place that attracts people. It's a place for your visitors to drop in, with opportunities for them to add thoughts with post-it notes, and ask questions. You can design it to be open at any time, or a place that has designated drop-in times. As the word itself suggests, this dedicated space is created to provoke thinking and an exchange of ideas, as well as a channel for you and your team to demonstrate what you're working on.

This space is also the ideal place to display your large journey maps and personas.

Retrospective

True to its definition, a 'retrospective' is about looking back. It served our species well in our hunting and gathering days when we told stories around the campfires of what worked, what didn't work, what presented danger and what provided safety. It was essential to our survival.

Ben Linders, an agile coach with a fabulous website of resources, provides this definition:

An agile retrospective is a practice used by teams to reflect on their way of working *and to **continuously become better** at what they do.*

Whilst not as critical for human survival today, the practice of a retrospective continues to provide great value. In an organisational context, a retrospective needs a facilitator who can help the group review their experiment or event, to discover what went well and what they can learn from the experience to improve it for next time. In turn, this promotes a culture of iterative learning.

Facilitate a retrospective, often called a *retro*, for your project team, as often as you need to, and focus on three key questions:
- What went well? Capture it so you don't forget it for next time. The good lessons are just as important as what we need to improve.
- What can be improved?
- What could/should we do differently next time?

Set up a flipchart like this one and provide an abundance of post-it notes so participants can contribute freely and anonymously:

THE RETROSPECTIVE

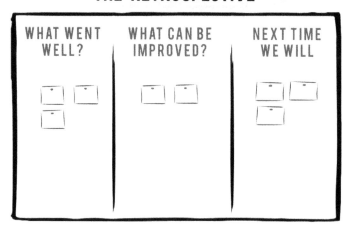

Compare this to a Post-Implementation Review (PIR), which is usually facilitated at the conclusion of the entire project to review numerous aspects of the initiative. In a project that's defined as 'agile', the retrospective is held at the end of each sprint or iteration, typically facilitated by the scrum master, so the learnings can be applied in the next sprint. On hybrid or waterfall projects, you can run a retro as often as you need to, as a shorter session, to focus on a particular aspect such as: *how did that session go for stakeholders?*

RETRO TIPS

- Set the scene so that it's a safe environment to reflect
- Allow everyone to have a voice
- Agree on next steps
- Assign actions and owners
- Schedule it for no longer than 60 minutes
- Take a photo of your retro flipchart
- Make your learnings visible to your stakeholders, considering your enterprise social network and visual management.

Small things can make a big difference. A client told me there was a great shift in her team by simply introducing three stand-up meetings each week. Another colleague told me that running retrospectives helped build a no-blame culture among team members, as they felt more comfortable talking about what didn't work so well.

When integrated into your change activities, these agile practices will foster trust and open conversations within and outside your team.

RELATED CHAPTERS: Change planning, Communicate to co-create

Agile practices can be applied in all your change planning and your day-to-day engagement with project team members, stakeholders and end users. The practices will promote deeper engagement and co-creation with your stakeholders. #changeessentials

29

CHANGE IS CHANGING

The accelerated speed of change demands an unprecedented agility to remain competitive. Conventional business models are vulnerable and no industry is exempt. Chaos has replaced certainty. The businesses failing to survive are the ones not seeing the signals, not adapting, or simply not keeping up with the pace of change. Just because something worked in the past, it does not guarantee repeat success. Business leaders can no longer look to the past for clues on how to manage the present, let alone the future.

This means that change is the new normal. It's no longer an event with a clear beginning, middle and end. Organisations know they need to change the way they plan, operate, execute, innovate and remain competitive. The answer for many is agile or new ways of working.

And new ways of working mean new ways of:
- Leading
- Thinking
- Behaving
- Learning
- Delivering change.

THE SANDS ARE SHIFTING

Two elements in our brave new world that are changing the way we work and have set the scene for agile ways of working are:

1 | The VUCA world

2 | New power.

1. THE VUCA WORLD

Businesses must become more proactively *adaptive*, or *agile,* to try things and learn from failure fast, deliver solutions to the customer more quickly, and take a truly human-centred design approach to product, service and nimble delivery.

This environment is now often referred to as VUCA (pronounced voo-ka). This acronym for *volatility, uncertainty, complexity* and *ambiguity* was coined by the US military back in the late 1990s, and has gained momentum in the last decade. It's now increasingly relevant in a business context, as decision making is becoming more complex.

So how do leaders stay up-to-date in a rapidly changing world? The conventional model of attending lengthy leadership programs and learning on the job or through coaching may not keep up with the calibre of skills needed to succeed in a VUCA environment. We need to continually build on our existing skills, refreshing our capability profile with the emerging capabilities required in a VUCA world.

VUCA CHARACTERISTICS

V

VOLATILITY
Unexpected or unstable circumstances, often of an unknown duration

U

UNCERTAINTY
A lack of predictability around the present situation and future outcomes

C

COMPLEXITY
Joining the dots is difficult due the range of multiple parts and variables

A

AMBIGUITY
With no precedents for what's happening, this is the place of the 'unknown unknowns'

Navigating VUCA

VUCA presents a paradox. Whilst we cannot predict the future based on the past, we need to make sense of it, accelerate our delivery, accept our failures as a learning experience and be sufficiently nimble to quickly adjust and improve through numerous short-cycle iterations.

Instead of shying away from a complex environment that's here to stay, we need to explore approaches that support our businesses and offer us insights into what we can do when we deliver change.

INTRODUCING THE VUCA PRIME

The *VUCA Prime*, developed by Bob Johansen, recommends that leaders provide *vision, understanding, clarity* and *agility* to minimise the impact of VUCA on decisions and actions.

THE VUCA PRIME
CONSIDERING VUCA ANTIDOTES

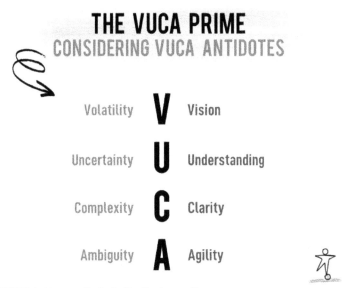

Volatility	**V**	Vision
Uncertainty	**U**	Understanding
Complexity	**C**	Clarity
Ambiguity	**A**	Agility

SOURCE: Bob Johansen, Centre for Creative Leadership

As an antidote to VUCA, the VUCA Prime provides clues to the capabilities required of change leaders and change managers, so they can turn the VUCA challenges into opportunities.

The VUCA Prime		CLUES FOR CHANGE PRACTITIONERS
V	VISION	Provide a clear vision of where the leaders see the organisation positioned in the next couple of years. Look for key message from leaders that articulate a vision, and communicate a clear intent that they plan to create a sustainable future.
U	UNDERSTANDING	To understand is to stop, look and listen beyond your area of expertise to make sense of the broader, competitive environment. By exploring practices and applications beyond the formal boundaries of your own business area or organisation, you are likely to discover new ways of thinking.
C	CLARITY	Look for what is known amidst the chaos. What does make sense? Use this information as 'anchors of certainty' that help provide clarity and stability for your impacted users, so they can make some sense of what appears to be chaos.

| A | AGILITY | Be nimble and adaptive so you can communicate across all levels. This involves letting go of hierarchical engagement models, with top-down cascaded communication, using the various available channels and networks, and adapting responses to unique situations as they arise. Provide clarity on the overall goals and vision, yet remain agile in the way you get there. |

2. NEW POWER

In a disruptive world, it's no surprise that the distribution of power, and the way power is exercised in a business environment, is also shifting. Traditional power, or old power, is challenged by digital, social networks, 24/7 connectivity and access to information. New power is challenging conventional approaches for communications and engagement, which rely on cascading information from the top down, as the prescribed way to vertically trickle information through organisational layers.

There are several external forces driving the shifts in power base - globalisation, generational skews towards millennials, digitalisation, multiple generations in the workplace, technology, and mobility, to name a few that are shaping the future of work.

In his TED talk titled *What new power looks like*, Jeremy Heimans used the table below to summarise the key trends. Since that TED talk in 2014, Jeremy Heimans and Henry Timms have published their book *New Power: How Power Works in Our Hyperconnected World*.

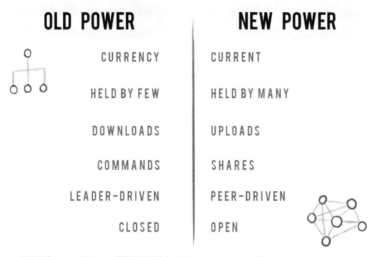

OLD POWER	NEW POWER
CURRENCY	CURRENT
HELD BY FEW	HELD BY MANY
DOWNLOADS	UPLOADS
COMMANDS	SHARES
LEADER-DRIVEN	PEER-DRIVEN
CLOSED	OPEN

SOURCE: Jeremy Heimans' TED Talk (2014): What new power looks like

The message here is clear. Traditional, hierarchical models of power in organisations are no longer hitting the mark in motivating the masses. A *command and control* approach is being replaced by connection and collaboration. Information, the commodity that was once restricted and served as a power base for senior executives, is now easier to access and share. Power and status are being disrupted and distributed, and agile behaviours are right for these new ways of leading, engaging and communicating with our teams.

CHANGE IS NO LONGER A PROCESS

As change practitioners, we have new challenges to navigate this brave new world where change is the new normal. Much of our methodology, frameworks and practice, up until now, has been based on theoretical change models that define change as a linear process. So what happens when our organisations, that are now in a constant state, change? A defined end state has less relevance in an environment that's continuously disrupted.

The VUCA environment and shifts in power dynamics demand that leaders and change practitioners continually refresh their capabilities. We need to stay current and to rethink our approach to how we advise on and support change. Change mastery is evolving and in the next few chapters we take a closer look at emergent practices that will serve change practitioners well.

HOW CHANGE IS CHANGING

For the last couple of years, I've been invited to speak or present on the future of change management. While we know the VUCA world is an uncertain one, I've made some predictions based on observations, deep conversations and experience. In my presentations I focus on three key messages to my audiences:

1. *The 'future of work' is here*

    We've been hearing about the *future of work* for some years. When we talk about the future, we are already priming our mindset for something that has not yet happened. This can cause inertia and delay at a time when we need to respond and adapt now, with a sense of urgency. The *future of work,* or that future we talk about, is already here. Embrace and model the new ways of working. The future of change management is *here* and *now*!

2. *The nature of our work is changing*

    It is estimated that 50-60 percent of change practitioners are employed as temporary contractors. As the workforce overall is becoming increasingly casualised, the change profession will be no exception. We can expect that our work will be more transient. In a more open employment market, also known as the *gig economy*, it's even more important to continue to refresh our skills to ensure we leave a positive imprint. What are you doing differently to your peers? How do you stand out? And how do you want to be remembered? Own your professional and personal development!

3.   *The capability paradox*

With continuous advances in technology, many manual or repetitive jobs are disappearing due to automation and new jobs are appearing. As a result, another acronym has entered our vocabulary - STEM. STEM stands for science, technology, engineering and mathematics. A great deal of research suggests that approximately three-quarters of all new jobs will need these STEM skills. Whilst I don't disagree with this forecast, I do worry that emphasis on human-centric skills doesn't attract the attention they deserve.

Despite the introduction of robotics, Artificial Intelligence and Machine Learning, the creation of new roles, and the automation of many tasks, organisations will continue to employ people. People need empathy, trust, involvement, and a sense of belonging with a human connection to thrive. Because change management is about how *people* embrace and adopt change, human-centred capabilities, such as emotional intelligence, are critical for roles in change management.

Successful change relies on co-creation and collaboration. By drawing on the disciplines of design thinking, behavioural science and human responses to change, we need to get better at facilitating conversations about how people are feeling and what they are thinking. In a time when we need to be more tech-savvy, we also need to nurture our human skills so we are people-savvy. Expectations in the workplace now mean that employees are considered internal clients, and the Employee Experience (EX) is being recognised as an important factor for engagement and retention.

FROM HERE TO THERE

Since presenting the future of change management, and observing the nature of our work in organisations, I've prepared an overview of the key shifts taking place in the actual work we do as change practitioners. While this diagram appears as two columns, it's not intended to be a dichotomy. Rather, it's a shift towards the right, or more activity is taking place on the right, and less is occurring on the left. Think of them as sliders that will vary depending on the change initiative in your organisation.

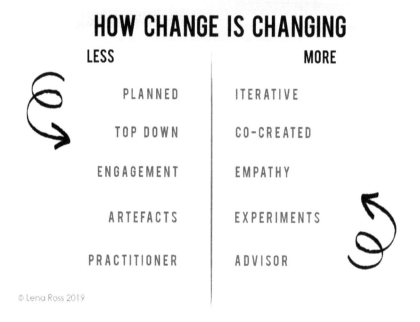

HOW CHANGE IS CHANGING

LESS	MORE
PLANNED	ITERATIVE
TOP DOWN	CO-CREATED
ENGAGEMENT	EMPATHY
ARTEFACTS	EXPERIMENTS
PRACTITIONER	ADVISOR

© Lena Ross 2019

Here's an overview of what these shifts mean:

LESS PLANNED, MORE ITERATIVE

I'm often asked for a process on how to deliver agile change. Because change is less event-based and more continuous, a planned approach is less relevant. There's a good reason why I open many of my workshops with this message, and feature the following quote by Richard Feynman. If you haven't heard of Mr Feynman, he was an American physicist and Nobel Prize winner. His brilliant approach to explain his work was matched by his charisma, and we now enjoy his legacy in the form of wonderful quotes such as this one:

Teach principles

not formulas

Richard Feynman

Working with principles instead of a prescribed formula is an approach that's aligned to new and agile ways of working. In an increasingly complex and ambiguous world, we need to draw on a range of tools and techniques so our work and change efforts are *fit for purpose*, while also promoting sense-making and co-creation. It's a mindset shift for many people as it means a departure from step-by-step methodologies and processes. By shifting to a more iterative approach that responds to what is needed in the moment, it opens more possibilities. It helps us approach change plans with a beginner's mindset, rather than assuming all change is planned and delivered in the same way. There is more on guiding principles for change management in the chapter titled *Agile change delivery*.

This shift represents a move away from following a change methodology that prescribes a list of artefacts to produce, towards change deliverables that are needed for each specific change, and being open to iteration as we progress.

LESS TOP-DOWN, MORE CO-CREATED

Until recently, our stakeholder engagement and communication plans were dictated by traditional power models based on hierarchy. We often planned a cascaded communication approach, to trickle down through organisational layers with little consideration for genuine two-way communication and buy-in.

While readiness surveys and engagement forums are designed to invite comments and feedback, they rarely provide an avenue for co-creation, where the change receivers' experiences are integrated into change activities and future state outcomes. The practice of design thinking, along with platforms for organic conversations across all business units and role titles, helps us engage to co-create.

LESS ENGAGEMENT, MORE EMPATHY

Empathy is deeper engagement because it means really understanding your end users. It's the ability to understand people's feelings and view their experience and pain points from various perspectives.

Conversations about feeling and thinking were once considered light and soft. But demonstrating empathy and vulnerability are now regarded as important qualities to build rapport and trust, enabling us to design change with a greater chance of success. In the chapter titled *Change management meets design thinking,* we explore empathy mapping and user journey mapping as tools to co-create the future state with empathy.

FEWER ARTEFACTS, MORE EXPERIMENTS

When I first started out in change management, the project plan was a Gantt chart that dictated a list of artefacts for the change team to complete, often before the change consultant was engaged to start the work. Large organisations with established project governance often prescribe a list of artefacts to be produced to meet their defined standards of best practice project and change management.

There is a shift away from this approach, as it's more important to produce work or documents that add value and drive meaningful conversations, rather than artefacts for the sake of ticking a box. Agile change delivery is about right-sizing your change activity, with an experimental approach that invites people to contribute and iterate. It's the scope and scale of your change initiative that helps you size your work, not the other way around with a list of prescribed artefacts.

LESS PRACTITIONER, MORE ADVISOR

When you start to right-size your change plans and effort for the change initiative, and experiment with different approaches to engage with your end users, your confidence will grow. A departure from a one-size-fits-all method means you will draw on a range of tools and practices to design a solution to suit the unique requirements of your organisation. This adaptive approach will signal a shift from being a toolkit-centred practitioner to a people-centred trusted advisor.

In our adaptation to new ways of working, there is a compelling need to demonstrate agility in our mindset, behaviours and practices.

 GOOD TO KNOW

In the brave new world, it's easy to see why and how our practice is evolving. The focus is on *emergent practice* rather than what we have been taught as *best practice*. With every change comes opportunity, and as change is constant, you will continually learn. We need to deliver change differently and engage our people in the spirit of co-creation and collaboration. It's exciting times for change practitioners, as your role will continue to evolve!

RELEVANT CHAPTERS: All the chapters in Agile Change Management and in this section on A Brave New World

#

The accelerated speed of change demands an unprecedented agility to remain competitive. Conventional business models are vulnerable and no industry is exempt. #changeessentials

#

Business leaders can no longer look to the past for clues on how to manage the present, let alone the future. #changeessentials

#

New power is challenging conventional approaches for communications and engagement, which rely on cascading information from the top down as the prescribed way to vertically trickle information through organisational layers. #changeessentials

#

In a time when we need to be more tech-savvy, we also need to nurture our human skills so we are people-savvy. #changeessentials

#

Agile change delivery is about right-sizing your change activity, with an experimental approach that invites people to contribute and iterate. #changeessentials

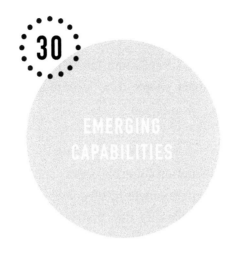

30

EMERGING
CAPABILITIES

In earlier chapters, we explored the core change capabilities such as change planning, stakeholder engagement and communications, along with assessing readiness and impacts. These capabilities and interventions have served us well for a long time. But now that change itself is changing, we need to build new capabilities that will equip us with skills for a disruptive business environment and ensure that our practice remains relevant.

By taking a future-forward view in how we deliver change, we will continue to add value to business success and benefits realisation. In the ongoing contribution we make to landing change in organisations successfully, the role of the change practitioner is constantly evolving.

We need to stay ahead of the curve!

This chapter explains four emerging capabilities and their relevance to change management. Each definition is presented as a change management capability, to explain how the capability would be demonstrated by someone performing the role of a change practitioner.

1. NEW WAYS OF WORKING

When we understand the trends and forces that are shaping the way we work, we can connect people to a purpose and the bigger picture macro-environment.

Why it's important

With a great deal of disruption going on, organisations have their focus on the external business environment to stay abreast of what their competitors are doing, and to identify new markets and emerging customer demands.

By closely watching trends that are disrupting the workplace around generations, technology, globalisation, learning, human resources, the gig economy, employee experience and mobility, we will be better positioned to understand how that disruption is affecting the way we work inside our own organisations. These same trends are shaping employee expectations in the way they interact with their employer, the space around them, the technology they use and how they collaborate with their team members.

And we know a positive employee experience is beneficial not just for the employees, but also for the organisation - it attracts and retains talent, and improves *productivity* overall and employee engagement.

Leading and communicating with people is demanding a new approach to resonate and deeply engage. With an understanding of the macro-environment in the world of work, particularly around new ways of working, we can continuously update our capabilities. This means we remain relevant and effective as change leaders and managers in motivating and retaining talented people.

How to use it

Link the objectives of your program or transformation to the bigger picture on how the workplace is changing, to connect your people to a higher purpose. This helps your narrative on the WHY.

Embrace the use of disruptive two-way communication channels in your organisation to promote and model co-creation and collaboration. Some of these are *Working out Loud, Enterprise Social Networks (ESNs)* such as *Yammer, Lean Coffee* and *Visual Management.*

RELATED CHAPTER: Communicate to co-create

2. DESIGN THINKING

Design thinking is a solution-focused and human-centred approach to creating the future for customers and employees.

Why it's important

Customers are setting a high bar with expectations that are being met by the disruptors (think Uber, AirBNB, Kogan, Amazon, Netflix... the list goes on). The pressure is on all businesses to be not only nimble and responsive to what the user wants, but also sufficiently innovative to create new demands.

Design thinking is used as a human-centred design practice to develop innovative solutions to everyday business challenges. The approach uncovers current and potential customer and end user pain points. Because a solution or new product usually translates to change, design thinking is now a much-needed skill in change management. Applying a human-centric lens to leading and managing change takes us to the very heart of what we do – to help our people adopt the change.

How to use it

Whilst human-centred design (HCD) is often applied to build empathy and solutions for our customers, the same thinking can be used to plan and introduce change. Consider your impacted employees as internal customers who can provide deep insights. Plan your change and identify post-implementation measures through the lens of what you want your people to do and think, and how you want them to feel.

Integrate HCD into your change plans and interventions to drive meaningful conversations with your stakeholders and impacted employees. Design employee journey maps to create a visual representation of the current and future state impacts. This is covered in more detail in the chapter in this section dedicated to design thinking.

Related chapter: Change management meets design thinking

3. DIGITAL LITERACY

Acquiring digital literacy means we can leverage various technology mediums to communicate, engage, co-create and learn, within and outside the organisation or business. It includes confidence with social media, particularly the use of enterprise social networks as communications and engagement channels. It also means we can demonstrate an understanding of digital trends such as data analytics, big data, machine learning, artificial intelligence (AI), the Internet of Things (IoT) and blockchain technology.

Why it's important

Outside the work environment, digital literacy enables you to find and share material on social media, and connect with like-minded people and industry networks outside your organisation, at a global level, to build an outside-in view.

In the workplace, integrating the use of social networks, collaboration tools, and other digital means of engaging helps us to become more efficient in our day-to-day work. Clever use of these digital channels enables faster and more effective co-creation, knowledge sharing and crowdsourcing solutions and information. You don't want technology evolving faster than your capacity or capability to adapt.

How to use it

In the workplace, change practitioners can lead and coach others in the use of digital channels, including social media, by modelling the behaviours and skills that need to be nurtured. For example, you can show that you are comfortable sharing information via less formal, digital channels, by engaging with colleagues and inviting feedback on enterprise social media platforms, back-channelling from events and workshops, and crowdsourcing ideas and solutions outside the formal communication channels to break through hierarchy and silos.

RELATED CHAPTERS: Agile change activity, Communicate to co-create

4. UNDERSTANDING HARDWIRED HUMAN BEHAVIOUR

With an ability to understand and consider the drivers of our hardwired responses to change, and how our cognitive biases can trip us up, we are better equipped to design change activity that is brain-friendly and less threatening.

Why it's important

The increased use of neuroimaging technology means that 90% of what we know about the brain has only been discovered in the last 10-12 years. New insights challenge our existing practice and encourage us to look at things with a fresh perspective. What we now know about our primal responses to threat and reward, along with our built-in biases, means we can lead change and prepare our people with an approach that's designed to minimise the threat response. We also know that the human response to change is not always resistance, yet our change plans often assume it is.

For a long time, organisations have understood the hidden costs of productivity dips and a disengaged workforce. Understanding hardwired human behaviour, through insights from neuroscience, can help us understand how and when discomfort occurs in the brain, hinting at techniques to optimise human performance.

How to use it

Find out more about what provokes the threat response, as that has a direct impact on human performance and productivity, and in turn, profitability.

Look for ways to reduce that threat response when you plan and deliver change. Consider whether stakeholders may perceive gain or loss as a result of the change.

For example, a top-down directive is likely to be less effective than two-way engagement where people feel involved, autonomous and a greater sense of fairness associated with changes. This is covered in more detail in the chapter titled *Brain-friendly change.*

RELATED CHAPTERS: Agile change activity, Brain-friendly change, Communicate to co-create

The interplay of the emerging capabilities

These much-needed change capabilities form an interrelated set of complementary skills. As the approach of business models moves from product-centric to customer-centric, design thinking principles are adopted to gain insights, along with an organisational appetite for rapid prototyping and delivery. A proficiency in digital channels enables us to analyse, communicate, and deploy effectively. To become better at putting our people - our customers and employees - at the heart of what we do is helped by an understanding of our hardwired behaviour and responses. This sophisticated interplay of capabilities will help us lead and implement change with a strong focus on collaboration and co-creation.

In your change practitioner role, ask yourself:
- How are we **defining** these capabilities in our business?
- How are we **building** these capabilities, at an individual, team and organisational level?

- How well do we **model** them?
- How do we **measure** them?
- How do we **reward** them?

💡 GOOD TO KNOW

We need to do things differently to lead and help others manage ongoing change. If you're not already building these emerging capabilities, now is the time to get started, because disruptive forces won't wait for you to catch up.

RELATED CHAPTERS: Change management meets design thinking, Brain-friendly change, Communicate to co-create, Staying ahead of the curve

With an understanding of the trends and forces that are shaping the way we work, we can connect people to a purpose and the bigger picture macro-environment. #changeessentials

Design thinking is a solution-focused and human-centred approach to create the future for customers and employees. #changeessentials

We need to do things differently to lead and help others manage ongoing change. If we're not already building new capabilities, now is the time to get started because disruptive forces won't wait for us to catch up. #changeessentials

31

CHANGE
MANAGEMENT MEETS
DESIGN THINKING

Design thinking is an *emerging capability* for change practitioners that enables us to take a deeper human-centred application to our change approach.

We're now leading and managing change in a disruptive environment, fraught with complexity and ambiguity. To quote Tim Brown, author of *Change by Design* and CEO of IDEO, Design thinking is defined as:

A discipline that uses the designer's sensibility and methods to match people's needs with what is technologically feasible and what a viable business strategy can convert into customer value and market opportunity.

It's worth pointing out that design thinking is often misunderstood to be a practice exclusively associated with art and design. The word 'design' can suggest that there is an artefact completed at the end of the process. In design thinking, the end result is not always a physical artefact, as one might expect an art and design student to produce.

The terms *design thinking* and *human-centred design (HCD)* are often used interchangeably. You may see these terms associated with user experience (UX), customer experience (CX), customer-centricity and systems thinking. Because a solution or new product usually translates to change, this is now a much-needed capability for leading and managing change.

As a framework, design thinking opens deep engagement with the end user, where the end result may be a new or improved product or service offering. It's a way of thinking that starts with the customer or end user.

DEFINING DESIGN THINKING

Design thinking helps us to create a human-centric culture of innovation, and transform insights into experiments that potentially become actionable ideas. Overall, it's about defining a problem to design a solution or product with the user in mind. The key principle is that the people who face the problems, or use the product, are the ones who can provide the most relevant insights and solutions.

Design thinking is as much about problem defining as it is about problem solving.

DEFINED AS A CHANGE CAPABILITY

For change practitioners, design thinking can be defined as:

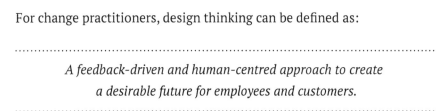

A feedback-driven and human-centred approach to create a desirable future for employees and customers.

A world famous design thinking school is the Hasso Plattner Institute of Design at Stanford, known as d.school. Here, you can attend public workshops to learn more by applying creative problem solving to real world problems.

D.school has developed a design thinking process that occurs in five iterative steps:

1 | Empathise

2 | Define

3 | Ideate

4 | Prototype

5 | Test.

Let's take a closer look at each of these five steps to find out:

1 | What it means

2 | How to apply it.

STEP 1: EMPATHISE

What it means

In the first step – **empathise** - we look for insights about the people for whom we are designing a product or service, or delivering change.

How to apply it

We learn about our users by watching them, engaging with them and immersing ourselves in their day-to-day life to understand their emotions. We listen to their stories, their pain points and their overall views to uncover the problem. To immerse ourselves, we need to try to 'walk a mile in their shoes'. This step is also referred to as *immersion* or *discovery*.

The information is often captured in a **persona**. The persona is a tool to help us learn more about our users. It's a *composite character* profile developed primarily for the purpose of improving the end user experience. A composite character is fictional, and draws on several real characteristics rather than one typical customer or user. As customer expectations are becoming higher, clever businesses are responding by developing customer-centric approaches in their product and service development. This means your persona is partly fictional and partly real, and considers *demographic* as well as *psychographic* characteristics.

For change initiatives, develop end user personas to represent your *impacted employees*. Include demographic elements such as age, gender, life cycle stage, where they live, and psychographic segmentation such as social preferences and lifestyle choices. In a work context, this would extend to work preferences, such as 'works part-time', and 'works remotely'.

Professionally built personas rely on extensive demographic and psychographic research to define an organisation's target market. Once patterns are identified after a series of one-on-one interviews, researchers or in-house interviewers will report on behaviours, motivation and attitude, to provide rich data for your development. If your organisation has invested in the preparation of customer personas, be sure to tap into that information for change initiatives that impact external customers, and for changes where your impacted employees may need to adjust their interaction with these customers.

The objective of the persona is to make your users more real and less ambiguous. It improves customer empathy as we have a 'person' to help us understand behaviour patterns and needs. Give each persona a name so he/she has an identity that resonates with the team.

On the next page is an example of a persona I used when developing the content for a workshop on hacking for agile change for change practitioners.

PERSONA

CHELSEA CHANGELING

BACKGROUND
- Change manager
- Works in the Central Business District (CBD) at the same company for four years
- Married with two children
- Started career in Human Resources, then worked as Change Analyst and was promoted to Change Manager

DEMOGRAPHICS
- Skews female
- Manager role
- Age 35
- Lives in suburban Melbourne

"I'd like to understand what I need to do as a Change Manager, when working on an agile project."

IDENTIFIERS
- Works as part of a project team
- Project managers in organisation are heading off to 'scrum training'
- Uses a well-known and respected global change methodology
- Many projects in the organisation are using a hybrid approach, i.e. waterfall and agile
- Is required to adopt agile practices in her change role, yet is unclear about what exactly that means

Another tool to investigate customer and user perspectives is an **empathy map**. This map is often represented in quadrants to capture emotions, pain points, gains and what the users are typically saying and doing *in their environment*. Another section I often add to empathy maps is space to prompt thinking on current and emerging trends, and how these may influence the way the end user will experience the product or service.

EMPATHY MAP

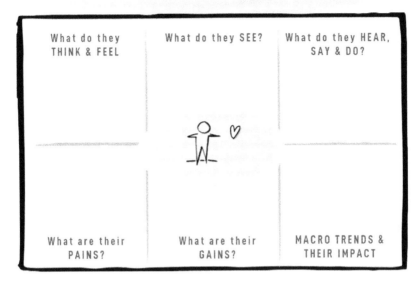

What do they THINK & FEEL

What do they SEE?

What do they HEAR, SAY & DO?

What are their PAINS?

What are their GAINS?

MACRO TRENDS & THEIR IMPACT

STEP 2: DEFINE

What it means

To **define** is to create a point of view that captures our insights on our users' needs: their point of view. We look for patterns that help us develop a problem statement or challenge to identify opportunities. This becomes the focal point for the next step, where we **ideate**.

How to apply it

Take your persona on a journey. Whether or not you compile a persona of your end users or customers, there is great value in scheduling time with your users to compile behavioural data using a **journey map**. This helps *define* a point of view: what your people are complaining about or fearing. What are their pain points in the *current* state? And how do you hope they will feel in the *future* state? We are looking to identify patterns in behaviour. Reframe pain points as *opportunities*.

The difference between a **journey map** and an **empathy map** is that the journey map explores greater detail by capturing the information in the phases of the user experience.

EMPLOYEE JOURNEY MAP

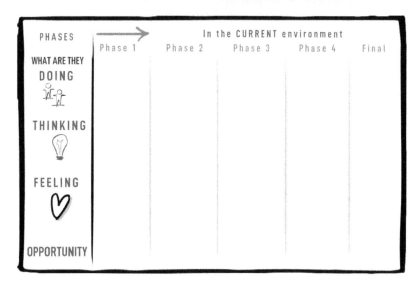

STEP 3: IDEATE

What it means

At the **ideate** step, we brainstorm with suspended judgement, to uncover a range of creative solutions to the problems and opportunities identified in the journey map. There are some ideation tips later in this chapter.

How to apply it

Ideation is about generating ideas to leverage divergent thinking and to challenge expected solutions. No doubt you've run or participated in numerous brainstorming sessions. Try to recall one or two of those sessions and think about how your ideas were recorded, or listened to. Which brainstorms were more successful, and why?

Be aware of your mindset. When we meet to gather ideas, we bring with us our experiences and pre-conceived ideas - in other words, our biases. Our experiences can be both a blessing and a curse. Whilst we bring great ideas through our own personal lens, it's incredibly hard to suspend judgement so we can simply observe without passing comment.

STEP 4: PROTOTYPE

What it means

When we **prototype**, we experiment by putting together a model or representation of the ideas to show others. Sometimes referred to as *rapid prototyping*, this is an inexpensive prototype with a *fail fast, learn fast* approach. We present back to our users and/or customers to gather feedback and to narrow or fine-tune options.

How to apply it

A prototype can be a storyboard, a rough sketch, a wall of post-it notes or a visual canvas. A clever prototyping technique is *bodystorming* - a process where the end users role-play as if they are in the future state. The purpose is to have something in a draft form in front of you, to drive a conversation with the end users you've already engaged, so you can look for what won't work. In this step, you can test more than one idea.

STEP 5: TEST

What it means

Testing is the time to refine the solution. Don't be surprised if this step leads to further iterations or takes you back to earlier steps to re-define and find out more about your users.

How to apply it

Test the prototype with a new user group. Walk them through it as if they are your first users. This will further test the improved version of your prototype that has taken into consideration the feedback you have gathered.

Depending on the change initiative being introduced, this step could involve revisions to a storyboard or visual canvas, a simulator environment, or a pilot workshop. The testing step may even take you back to the empathy map or journey map, as you may gain new insights.

THE INTERSECTION

Applying the design thinking lens sharpens our focus to the people side of our change practice, taking us back to the very heart of what we do: we help our people adopt the change. Design thinking therefore becomes a valuable part of our toolkit for developing change plans. In using it, we show our clients and project teams that we align our capability and value as change leaders and professionals to the changing demands of the business environment.

The design thinking approach helps us discover, define, review and iterate our change approach with the user experience in mind. Spending time at the beginning to identify the people issues, the experience *now* and what it *could be* helps us identify post-implementation metrics.

Design thinking is often applied for customer personas and developing empathy for our customers, but we can see the value of applying the same approach to introduce change. Considering our impacted employees as internal customers provides deep insights and drives meaningful conversations with our stakeholders and impacted people.

💡 GOOD TO KNOW

An important benefit for change practitioners is that when you apply design thinking practices, such as running workshops on journey maps, you create a safe place for people to talk about feelings and thoughts.

Design thinking legitimises a conversation about emotions that may not occur otherwise.

Now that I've used design thinking practices in my change approach, I can't imagine doing it any other way.

There's a great deal of information available. IDEO, Frog Design and d.school have great resources on their websites, referenced at the end of this book. You can also check out a clip where I talk to Dr Gene Bawden, Head of Monash Art, Design and Architecture (MADA) at Monash University.

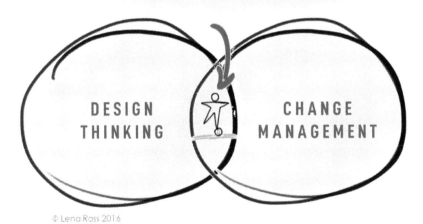

Design thinking is used as a human-centred practice to define problems first, in order to develop innovative solutions to everyday business challenges. So you could say that where design thinking meets change management is the real sweet spot!

RELEVANT CHAPTERS: Change measures, Emerging capabilities

Design thinking is as much about problem defining as it is about problem solving. #changeessentials

When change practitioners apply design thinking practices such as running workshops on journey maps, an important benefit is the creation of a safe place for people to talk about feelings and thoughts. It legitimises a conversation about emotions that may not occur otherwise. #changeessentials

The design thinking approach helps us discover, define, review and iterate our change approach with the user experience in mind. Spending time at the beginning to identify the people issues, the experience *now* and what it *could be* helps us identify post-implementation metrics. #changeessentials

32

BRAIN-FRIENDLY CHANGE

In the last decade, new insights from the field of brain science, also known as *neuroscience*, have taught us a great deal about our primal behaviour and the human response to change. A deeper understanding of our hardwired behaviour and emotional responses helps us plan and deliver change in a way that resonates with our primal instincts. It helps us understand how change impacts human performance and how we can get the best out of ourselves and the *people* we lead.

The more we know about how we are hardwired to respond, the more we can do to make change stick!

Knowing more about how our brain processes change and filters new information, nudges us to reconsider our assumptions that people will naturally resist change. Our change plans and interventions usually assume resistance, but the human response ranges from acceptance and support to resistance. The key is to find out why the *same change* can trigger a range of experiences and emotional responses.

CHANGE IS NOW AN ART AND A SCIENCE

Until very recently, the discipline of change management fell neatly in the category of social science. Whilst social science traditionally explores the human mind and behaviour through observation and conclusion, neuroscience studies the anatomy and physiology of the brain and can observe responses with imaging technology. Before we delve into what this means for change management, let's take a closer look at what the field of neuroscience is revealing.

Dr David Rock, a key Australian researcher in this field, has helped bring together the disciplines of neuroscience and behavioural science and coined the term *NeuroLeadership,* which is made up of four domains:

1 | Decision making and problem solving

2 | Emotional regulation

3 | Collaboration and influence

4 | Change leadership.

Along with other neuroscientists, David Rock has used brain-based research and imaging technology to compile scientific data to complement earlier behavioural studies. Simply put, they've added a hard edge to what is often considered a soft science, whilst providing new insights into effective leadership and inspiring employee engagement.

LOSS EQUATES TO THREAT

Our response to loss is elegantly expressed in David Rock's SCARF model of threat and reward.

SCARF stands for:

S – Status

C – Certainty

A - Autonomy

R - Relatedness

F – Fairness.

In his PhD research, David Rock discovered that when one or more elements in the SCARF model are reduced or taken away, our brain activates a threat response. If we perceive we are gaining in one or more of the SCARF elements, we experience a reward response.

Here's how each element of the SCARF model relates to our responses to change and new information:

STATUS

We have a hard-wired social need for respect, esteem and a place in a 'pecking order'. A perception of one's status being lowered will trigger the threat response, which is similar to a primal threat to one's safety. When status is threatened, people may defend a position that doesn't make sense, to avoid their perceived pain or drop in status.

CERTAINTY

We like to know what will happen next. When an unfamiliar or new situation is presented, the brain is confused and works overtime to make sense of the situation, taking up more neural energy. When uncertainty increases, memory and commitment decline. This validates many existing change models that acknowledge a period of lower productivity during times of transformation.

AUTONOMY

The opportunity to make choices or to exercise some control over one's environment also increases the sense of certainty, therefore reducing stress. Allowing people to make autonomous decisions increases motivation and engagement, but a leader who micro-manages will have the opposite effect. Even the perception of autonomy is important!

RELATEDNESS

We need to feel safe around people in our group/s. Social connection is a primal need. The brain is programmed to classify a person as 'friend' or 'foe'. The 'foe' triggers a threat response. Interestingly, social neuroscientists have found that social exclusion creates the same neural response as physical pain. This means social pain is like physical pain.

FAIRNESS

An experience of unfairness, even if only a perception, will result in less productivity and more negativity, registering the same brain response as a physical pain. Fairness is perceived in relative terms. For example, even if not motivated by financial rewards, people will regard the situation as unfair if they feel they are underpaid relative to their peers. Yet a perceived improvement in fairness activates the same neural response as receiving a monetary reward or eating chocolate.

THE SCARF MODEL
OF SOCIAL THREATS AND REWARDS

S   **STATUS**
About relative importance to others

C   **CERTAINTY**
Concerns about being able to predict the future

A   **AUTONOMY**
A sense of control over events

R   **RELATEDNESS**
A sense of safety with others

F   **FAIRNESS**
A perception of fair exchanges between people

SOURCE: Rock, D & Schwartz, J. (2006) The neuroscience of leadership

Okay, we know that models are great in theory, but how can we use this information in practice, in organisations?

I often facilitate sessions for teams about to experience change, particularly organisational change. After a brief introduction to Rock's SCARF model, and how change is the new normal these days, we typically brainstorm how team members felt impacted by each SCARF element. To capture this, I have developed a self-assessment tool (see sample below) for them to plot how they felt on a SCARF threat/reward scale. We then collate each team member's rating on a flipchart sheet, to get a picture of the extent of the team's pain points in terms of each SCARF element. This helps the team to label their feelings through awareness, and it drives a productive discussion on how they will manage the challenges ahead as a group.

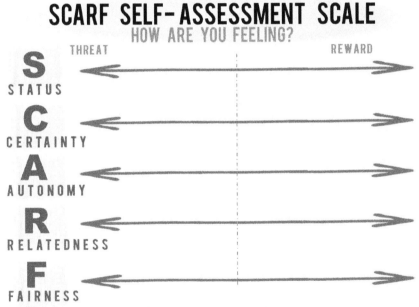

SCARF SELF-ASSESSMENT SCALE
HOW ARE YOU FEELING?

THREAT   REWARD

S
STATUS

C
CERTAINTY

A
AUTONOMY

R
RELATEDNESS

F
FAIRNESS

SOURCE: Designed by Lena Ross (2012) based on David Rock's SCARF model

We can also apply the SCARF model as a framework for planning and delivering change. For example, we can assess the anticipated threat response of each stakeholder for each element of SCARF, educate our change champions on how it plays out, and consider how we frame our communication, train and generally prepare people for changes.

SO WHAT DOES THIS MEAN FOR CHANGE PRACTITIONERS?

Brainstorm tips on how to reduce the threat response with your leadership teams. You can build on this table with your own ideas, to make it relevant to your workplace culture and change scenario:

Emotional Driver	Ways to Reduce Threat
STATUS *About relative importance to others*	Seek out subject matter expert feedback and acknowledge it. If a team member's status is impacted by the change, find another way to reward them that gives them recognition within the group.
CERTAINTY *Concerns about being able to predict the future*	If you can't communicate details, let people know when more information will become available to provide anchor points of certainty. Establish and share future-state journey maps. Discuss rumours openly. Provide a forum for rumour busting.
AUTONOMY *Provides a sense of control over events*	Provide a broad picture of the change and ask others how it could work. Establish a network of change champions who become peer advocates. Provide channels for self-directed learning opportunities to provide options.
RELATEDNESS *A sense of safety with others*	Support enterprise social networks as a communication channel to provide a sense of 'community'. Show vulnerability and acknowledge any shortcomings or areas for improvement in the change approach and what you've learned from it.
FAIRNESS *A perception of fair exchanges between people*	Be clear and transparent about how decisions will be made. Provide many opportunities for people to have their say, so all have access to information and involvement.

Source: My white paper on the neuroscience of change (found on my website) titled Navigating through transformation: A neuroscience based toolkit for change, *2014.*

SO WHAT DOES THIS MEAN FOR LEADERS?

As disruption continues to demand unprecedented agility to remain competitive, these insights from neuroscience offer organisations a clear *value proposition*. The application of these findings can only improve business success. Minimising threat means a more engaged workforce. And we know engaged workers are more productive and less resistant to change, so business benefits can be realised faster from transformation efforts.

These new insights challenge our existing practices and encourage us to look at things with a fresh perspective. What we now know about our hardwired responses to threat (change and potential change) means it's time to review leadership and change practices, the way we frame communication and engage our stakeholders, as well as our overall change experiments. It provokes us to think harder about how to reduce the 'pain' our people experience when introduced to change.

 GOOD TO KNOW

As mentioned earlier in this chapter, the more we know about how we are hardwired to respond, the more we can do to **make change stick!** It's worth taking the time to find out what provokes a threat response and take steps to reduce it.

Now that we can observe and measure neural activity responses to new information and events, we can confidently reposition the 'soft science' of change management as a 'hard science'.

RELATED CHAPTERS: Change myths, Change resistance, Change fatigue

As disruption continues to demand unprecedented agility to remain competitive, insights such as these from neuroscience offer organisations a clear *value proposition*. Minimising threat means a more engaged workforce. And we know engaged workers are more productive and less resistant to change, so business benefits can be realised faster from transformation efforts. #changeessentials

The more we know about our hardwired responses to threat, the better we can frame communication, engagement of our stakeholders, and our overall change experiments. It provokes us to think harder about how to reduce the 'pain' our people experience when introduced to change. #changeessentials

Now that we can observe and measure neural activity responses to new information and events, we can confidently reposition the 'soft science' of change management as a 'hard science'. #changeessentials

33

COMMUNICATE TO CO-CREATE

We've explored the planning and execution of conventional change communications. As power is being redefined and shifting, the way we communicate and influence is changing. Change managers and leaders need to tap into new and different communication channels to achieve two key objectives:

1 | To inform

2 | To engage.

The newer communication channels are sometimes considered disruptive because they differ from the power-based and top-down approaches. Here are some more ways in which small things can make a big difference!

The conventional change communication approach relies on top-down communication, which is one-way, and often delivered by a senior employee who has formal influence and power in the organisation. We often see the 'cascade' approach where messages are trickled down, layer by layer, from the executive team. This type of communication continues to play a role in communicating change to *inform* and to demonstrate endorsement and support of the initiative. Rarely, however, does it invite organic feedback or engagement.

Participatory two-way communication both *informs* and *engages* the audience. It invites conversation and creates opportunity for involvement and co-creation. And what a great way to uncover your potential change advocates!

REACHING YOUR AUDIENCE

If you take into account the overwhelming amount of information you receive and process each day, you need to be creative about the messages that reach your audience. The approach of top-down communication - typically via email - is fast being regarded as hierarchical, visually dull and linear. The effectiveness of email is likely to diminish in favour of more participatory methods.

The newer channels of two-way communication are reshaping the way we lead, communicate and interact in organisations. Demographic forecasting tells us that by 2025, millennials will make up 75 percent of the workforce. As digital natives, this generation is engaging and gathering information through online platforms that invite two-way dialogue, making email communication less relevant.

Here are four communication channels that promote co-creation which you can use in your workplace right now - *Enterprise Social Networks* (ESNs), *Lean Coffee, Visual Management and Working Out Loud.*

1. ENTERPRISE SOCIAL NETWORKS (ESNS)

An enterprise social network (ESN) is a platform used in organisations to facilitate online communication and collaboration. A leading ESN used in the workplace is Microsoft-owned Yammer. Slack, Jive, SocialCast and Microsoft Teams are also popular. If you're not already familiar with ESNs, think of it as a Facebook for the workplace. If you are of the mindset that an ESN is not formal enough to rate as a communication channel, it's time to watch business trends. It's the *informality* of an ESN that makes it effective and a must-have in your toolkit.

Use your ESN as a communication channel for updates, uploading photographs of visual management boards and events, inviting comments, promoting events coming up, sharing relevant news articles and your own expertise and knowledge, floating your ideas, crowdsourcing solutions to problems, or asking for support or expertise to help you. You can even use this channel to carry out short online polls for a quick pulse check.

With ESNs come numerous other benefits such as breaking down silos and geographical barriers, so you can establish connections across divisions while providing a two-way communications channel that isn't top-down – a real accelerator for co-creation that cannot be overlooked.

ESNs are being adopted by more and more leaders and change practitioners across numerous organisations as critical communications and engagement channels, making the ESN one of the most accessible and effective culture hack tools on hand. In the past, centralised knowledge created a power base, often in the hands of leaders who would decide when to release it. These social networking channels have dismantled the ivory tower of information and engagement, making knowledge available faster and providing opportunities for everyone to collaborate across divisions, from CEO to the 'shop floor'. Everyone has a voice and the opportunity to make a difference.

ESNs have disrupted old, formal power. Through ESN platforms, information is created, shared and distributed by many, rather than by a few who control a traditional top-down, cascaded communication.

2. LEAN COFFEE

A discussion about two-way communication in an agile environment is not complete without a commentary on the concept of Lean Coffee. It claims its roots in Seattle back in 2009 when a couple of agile thought leaders, Jim Benson and Jeremy Lightsmith, wanted to start a group of like-minded people. Its purpose at the time was to meet informally to discuss lean techniques, in the spirit of collaborative learning. The concept of Lean Coffee was born... and took off.

Lean Coffee is a democratic meeting with some structure and no agenda. Participants gather and decide on the agenda together. This approach is ideal for groups of up to 12 people. With lean principles in mind, the structure is minimal. Here's how it works:

1 | Schedule a meeting. Pique interest by calling it Lean Coffee.

2 | Be sure to take post-it notes and have a wall or flipchart stand handy.

3 | Set up a different version of a Kanban board to show the progress of the meeting, with these three suggested headings: To Discuss, Discussing, Discussed.

4 | Attendees write on post-it notes the topics they want to discuss, and place them in the To Discuss column. Encourage as many ideas possible.

5 | Allow each person to introduce their topic in one or two sentences.

6 | Each participant gets two votes. You can vote twice for the same thing, or one vote per topic, by placing a dot or tick next to the one you support.

7 | Start with the topics with the most votes.

8 | Take a photo of all the topic cards in case you need to revisit them in another session.

LEAN COFFEE
EXAMPLE OF OPEN INVITATION

Join us for **LEAN COFFEE**
This is an informal session where we will discuss the new change framework and approach.
It will be structured so you determine the agenda.

WHERE?
Level 8 open café
area

CONTACT?
Lena Ross
<email address>

WHEN?
Monday 15 March
10.00am

No RSVP needed
Just rock up!

WHAT to BRING
An open mind!

3. VISUAL MANAGEMENT

Our brains process visual information faster by processing multiple images at the one time. For too long, we've been inundated with text-based pages of PowerPoint slides. As attention spans become shorter, and we are overwhelmed with mountains of information from various sources, we need to be clever about how we communicate and capture information.

Visual management boards can be openly displayed in the workplace to communicate progress of work, along with dashboard-style representations of business measures and targets achieved. Because of their visibility, these boards open conversation informally, in both scheduled meetings and through ad hoc, unscheduled chats. As agile practices like stand-up meetings continue to grow, so is the use of visual management boards as a source of status updates, stories, 'strategies on a page', and work in progress.

Visually compelling messages create a real WOW factor, setting a new expectation in how information is communicated. The good news is that you don't need to be a gifted artist or calligrapher. There are some effective infographic packages online where you can experiment with a limited range of templates for free. Look for *Canva* and *Piktochart* to get started.

Some messages need to be delivered or captured in real time. So it is **even better** if you can record and deliver information using the power of humble chunky markers and flipchart paper.

An effective way to communicate the story of your change initiative to your stakeholders, and more broadly across the organisation, is to animate your story. You can outsource this and have it completed in just a couple of weeks. Check out FLIMP Studios, an organisation that is very clever at creating change posters, interactive PDF documents and animated videos that communicate key messages in an engaging way. You can watch samples of their clips on the FLIMP Studios website, listed in my references.

Show your work on an experience wall

An effective way to visually broadcast your change initiative, progress and key activity is on an experience wall. Find a space you can use that is located close to the project team. If space is scarce, one or two mobile whiteboards can create the same impact.

An experience wall will:
- Showcase visual elements of the program
- Form part of the engagement approach
- Be a place for your personas to live
- Provide a space to work out loud, show your work
- Promote awareness and invite feedback
- Help initiate conversations
- Feature in pictures on your enterprise social network.

When you feature your Kanban Board on your visual board, it's also a good place for your team to congregate for stand-up meetings. This alone can become a talking point with stakeholders; it further demonstrates what the team is working on and is consistent with agile ways of working.

 GOOD TO KNOW

If you are questioned on the value of visual management boards as a powerful communication channel, it may be helpful to remind your stakeholders or project team members that the human brain processes visual information 60,000 times faster than text. You can build a convincing case based on this information!

4. WORKING OUT LOUD

Working out loud (often abbreviated to WOL) is growing in popularity due to its simplicity and effectiveness in promoting engagement and co-creation. It's the practice of doing your work in a way that is visible to your colleagues. By working openly, you have the opportunity of gathering additional information and possibly avoiding duplication of effort. How many times have you started research or prepared documentation, only to find out later that someone else has completed something similar that could have saved you hours of duplicated work? The benefits in working out loud are immediate and easy to see.

The term WOL was first coined in 2011 by Bryce Williams, a social collaboration specialist, when he used it to define work that is observable to others. WOL advocate John Stepper has written numerous blogs on this practice, and more recently a book. Stepper has identified five elements to truly define working out loud. WOL:

1 | *Makes your work visible.*

2 | *Makes work better.* Seek ways to improve your work through feedback and discussion.

3 | *Leads with generosity.* Share your work in progress with others, not just for engagement, but also because the discussions will help you discover other work underway and specialist skills you can tap into.

4 | *Builds a social network.* As you continue to work out loud, you will connect with more like-minded people who are likely to become part of your personal learning network; if you are leading or managing a change, you will find supporters and champions.

5 | *Makes your work purposeful.* Identify your purpose and be transparent about it.

I find out interesting and unexpected things when I work out loud. On one occasion, I placed a post on the organisation's *Yammer* channel inviting people to drop into a room I had booked out for a day, to see a capability uplift program I was developing. The purpose was to provide visibility on my work and to invite input on the content they were hoping to learn. Because our *Yammer* group had attracted numerous members outside our immediate team, the post attracted more interest than my initial target group. The result was that by working out loud, I uncovered a broader interest; and we were able to join forces with other business units to develop richer content with greater relevance for our audience. This prevented what could have been duplication of effort in other business areas. It also introduced diversity of thought. What a great way to hack across organisational silos!

WORKING OUT LOUD

Lena is working out loud so please drop in:
MONDAY 1-4pm
WEDNESDAY 9am-12pm

It's a rapid way to gather feedback and invite discussion. People become engaged when they have an opportunity for involvement, and working out loud provides a non-threatening channel for co-creation. The perfect aid for working out loud is your ESN. This is the fastest and most effective way to announce what you are creating.

There's a great deal of information and many blogs on these *four channels* for you to explore further. Changing the way we work and communicate is making us better at what we do. Co-creation can mean a shift in mindset, as it demands the willingness and courage for transparency, along with confidence with social media - all capabilities we can build through practice and experience. These four communication channels take a rapid and sometimes cheeky angle to get the message through, but overall they carry the honourable intent of engagement and involvement.

RELATED CHAPTERS: Change communication, Change is changing, Agile change activity

#

As power is being redefined and shifting, the way we communicate and influence is changing. Change managers and leaders need to tap into additional new and different communication channels to engage and invite collaboration. #changeessentials

#

Our brains process visual information 60,000 times faster than text. #changeessentials

34

STAYING AHEAD OF THE CURVE

There are numerous 'forces' at play that are reshaping the work environment. Firstly, there are the game changers driven by numerous disruptive factors in the external environment, such as digitisation, technology, mobilisation and automation. At the same time, we have a *gig economy* – a term frequently used to describe the increase in the number of independent contractors and consultants employed in organisations as knowledge workers on short-term engagements. These freelancers work side-by-side with permanent staff.

Change practitioners employed as permanent employees may be fortunate enough to receive some professional development through their employer. However, a high percentage of change practitioners are contractors, and unlikely to receive funded training as part of their engagement.

The accelerated rate of change means we need to future-proof our skills and knowledge, so that we can remain current, relevant and most of all, adaptable.

In this landscape, employees - especially contractors - have a greater responsibility to drive and build their own capability through various learning channels. With an abundance of information available from various sources, a great deal of learning can take place at little or no cost. However, to explore these opportunities and self-direct our professional and personal development, we do need a learning or growth mindset.

LEARNING BEYOND CLASSROOM TRAINING

A common way to learn is via face-to-face training sessions. However, if you want to be abreast of industry trends, there are various ways to continue learning as well as maintain connection with your industry best practice and peers. In other words, it requires *self-directed learning*. Consider these self-directed learning channels:

- Social learning
- Experimenting
- Microlearning
- Multiple channels.

Social learning

Historically, the formal teacher-centric classroom is a relatively recent invention as a learning channel. A place where there is often one-way communication, and little tolerance for debate and noise, is not a fertile ground for productive discussion and self-discovery. We humans have spent most of our time on this planet learning through observation, oral history, and storytelling with our tribes, and further shared our skills, wisdom and knowledge beyond our close flock at larger clan gatherings. We learn faster and more effectively from our peers.

Just as we are hardwired to connect with others, the same goes for how we learn best. We are innately social beings who are also rewarded when we discover new things on our own. The 'aha' moment, when we connect key learnings to our own experiences and 'join our own dots', activates a reward centre in the brain. Social learning, through observation and participation with others, is just how our brains are designed to learn.

We learn a great deal by *observation*. This is often underestimated, as we are conditioned to believe that most of our learning occurs in a classroom.

Social learning is learning by sharing our knowledge and expertise through observation, social interaction and connection.

Experimenting

Do you remember when you first created your Facebook, LinkedIn or Instagram accounts? Did you go to a classroom to learn how, or did you play around to work it out? Perhaps you sourced some tips from friends? Chances are there was no formal learning event and you learned by doing. If we stop to consider how much we have learned, especially in the last 20 years with digital tools, we should be proud of the change we've adopted and skills we've self-taught in both our professional and personal lives.

Microlearning

Microlearning is learning through shorter and sharper activities or experiences. Think of blogs, podcasts or short clips on social media. Because most microlearning is available through multiple digital channels, we can learn anytime, anywhere. Our brains like choices and options. Offering this level of autonomy to learners activates a reward response in the brain, making it more likely that they will participate in a learning activity.

If you consider what you've learned in the last 12-24 months, and how you've acquired the new information, chances are high that a great deal of it has been through less formal learning, and in very small bites.

MULTIPLE CHANNELS

Find your learning village

Meetups, industry networking events and conferences provide an ideal social learning environment. In the one forum you get the latest thinking in your field, most of which isn't even published in books yet. The agenda is carefully planned to bring you the latest and best. It's the modern version of a clan gathering, where the intersection of networking and learning takes place in an environment of focus and commitment. People have suspended their day-to-day activity in pursuit of social connection and information, delivered mostly in a non-hierarchical forum.

SELF-DIRECTED LEARNING

Remember the autodidact - the self-taught person referred to in the earlier chapter on Agile change delivery? Here are some ways to explore self-directed learning:

- MOOCs
- TED talks
- YouTube and Vimeo
- LinkedIn and LI groups
- Conferences
- Webinars.

GET IN THE DRIVER'S SEAT

Social media and access to online learning and networks have made it easier than ever before to stay ahead of the curve in your field. We know that organisations are spending less on formal training budgets; in particular, permanent employees are being replaced by contractors. This places a greater importance on directing your learning through developing your *Personal Learning Network (PLN),* to navigate disruptive times and to continue to grow.

Developing a PLN signals an intention to learn, with an understanding that much of the learning will take place organically. This type of mindfulness applied to your learning will enhance your capability.

A personal learning network is your informal (outside of a classroom and books) learning network, where you learn from various sources and through numerous channels. By connecting with a range of people, you will tap into different perspectives and fresh insights; and as with any curious journey, you will discover the unexpected. You probably already have a form of a PLN, but it's worth working on it to expand your reach.

A PLN is based on the principle of *paying it forward*, which means that you may not always *repay* the person or source who helped you, but you share your learning with someone else. The added benefit is that when you help others learn, you learn more, which is based on the assumption that you are motivated to learn more about your topic when you are sharing your knowledge with others.

The concept of learning through a vast network ties in neatly with how we are hardwired to connect and learn. Try drawing your own PLN, like the one below, and see what you come up with.

PERSONAL LEARNING NETWORK

© Lena Ross, 2015

OWN YOUR CAPABILITY

Now that we can easily connect and learn through the plethora of online channels from TED talks to social networks such as Twitter and LinkedIn, it's an ideal time for you to carve your path of self-directed learning. Staying abreast of industry trends requires dedicated effort. Be creative when thinking about your development. While formal training is suitable in some cases, often the best approach is to throw yourself into a task, project or role that you've never done before.

 GOOD TO KNOW

Self-directed learning is your way to acquire information, just in time, when you need it, and to stay ahead of the curve!

The more that you read,

the more things you'll know.

The more that you learn,

the more places you'll go!

Dr Seuss

RELATED CHAPTERS: Roles in change management, Change capabilities

Self-directed learning is your way to acquire information, just in time, when you need it, and to stay ahead of the curve. #changeessentials

35

WHAT'S NEXT?

With so much information available from so many sources, it's easy to be overwhelmed. Keep in mind that there is no one way, or right way, to approach change management - it draws on various disciplines and stays true to human-centred design principles.

Let's revisit one of my favourite quotes by Richard Feynman: *teach principles not formulas*. I often refer to this quote in my workshops on agile and new ways of working. I like it because in our world of uncertainty and ambiguity, we need guiding principles more than rigid or step-by-step processes. While this book has provided a great deal of information on templates and approaches, it is not a prescribed approach to change management. It is designed to equip you with knowledge of change capabilities, what they look like, and how you can demonstrate value as a change practitioner.

Each organisation has different characteristics in nuances, culture and industry type; and each will be best served by a change plan and approach that is right for them in size and nature at that point in time. The art of a good change consultant is to recognise the unique characteristics of both the organisation and the project, and to devise a plan that stays true to the principles yet is adaptive in its development and delivery.

This means that the role of the change practitioner is an emerging and changing role, and it demands a nimble approach to meet the ongoing challenges faced by organisations. Whilst the future of change management as a practice looks optimistic, the relevant industry associations need to focus on ongoing professional development for their members, to transform these challenges into opportunities.

💡 GOOD TO KNOW

The hallmark strength of humanistic values will not lose its relevance. It can be applied to newer approaches, such as agile ways of working, equally as well as it has been applied in the past. Just as organisations and leaders need to be nimble to succeed, change practitioners will need to be equally resilient and adaptive to thrive in our brave new world.

IT'S LIKE A SUSHI TRAIN

We could ruminate for hours, or even days, on what makes a good change practitioner. We know that attending a course doesn't make a good change manager, just as spending hours in a garage won't make you a competent motor car mechanic. It's the practice and experience that build the confidence and capability to know what to do and when to apply it.

Remember the concept of the sushi train mentioned earlier in the book? If you don't need a tool or practice for today's change initiative, it remains on the train, ready for you to pick up if you need it on your next assignment.

Make sure you keep this book on your sushi train, so you can pick it up when you need to! ☺

PARTING WORDS

While we've arrived at the end of the book, this is SO NOT the end. It's just the beginning.

I ask my clients and workshop participants to think about it as the *thin end of the wedge*. A learning event, such as attending a workshop or reading a book, is not conclusive in itself. Just as a wedge widens, acquiring new information should provoke more thinking, nudge curiosity, and create excitement for the continued learning and experimenting ahead.

And... one more poignant quote from that American physicist:

The more you know,

The more you know

What you don't know

Richard Feynman

#

The role of the change practitioner is an emerging and changing role, and it demands a nimble approach to meet the ongoing challenges faced by organisations. #changeessentials

THE BOY AND THE HAZELNUTS

The boy put his hand into a pot full of hazelnuts.

He grasped as many as he could possibly hold, but when he tried to pull out his hand, he was prevented from doing so by the neck of the pot.

Unwilling to lose his hazelnuts, and yet unable to withdraw his hand, he burst into tears and bitterly lamented his disappointment.

Lesson: Do not attempt too much at once

SOURCE: Aesop's Fables

TABLE OF 'GOOD TO
KNOW' SNIPPETS

	Chapter	Good to know
1	**Introduction**	Throughout this book the terms *change managers, change practitioners* and *change consultants* mean the same thing.
2	**Getting into change management**	The best approach in your resume is to keep the language simple and explain any acronyms you use. Look for opportunities to align the language with words in the job advert or role description.
		Don't be baffled by terminology, as consistency in language in the change management profession across organisations and the globe is not an exact science!
		• For example, a *change agent* in one organisation may mean a change manager, whilst in another business, it means a champion of change. Variation in terminology can confuse not only the change consultants who work across different organisations, but also the people within the business who will be impacted by the change.
		• Be comfortable with your own understanding of a change practitioner to help you get past varied definitions across organisations and countries.
		• You may hear change referred to as the 'delta'. For example, someone may say to you what's the delta? If you haven't heard this term before, it's quite confusing.

	Chapter	Good to know
		• Delta, the fourth letter of the Greek alphabet, is also represented as a triangle, like this △. It's also the mathematical symbol for 'variation', so it's now sometimes used to mean the word 'change'. You might even see 'change' abbreviated to the triangle, eg △ management.
3	**Types of change**	It's worth noting that for change practitioners engaged on organisational change programs, particularly where redundancies are involved, the work can take an emotional toll. Be mindful of how the emotional responses of others may impact you, so that you can take good care of yourself. Self-care is essential!
		Each type of change initiative usually occurs for a specific reason, and is often caused by activity in the external business environment.
		You may hear the term *BaU change* or *Business as Usual change* as a contrast to change initiatives that are delivered by a dedicated project team.
		BaU change is change that occurs frequently and usually on a small scale, within business units, as part of their operations. This type of change is managed by the business, most often without additional or dedicated change practitioners. It may involve a process change or the introduction of new policy, for example, the introduction of 'working from home' policies or guidelines is a BaU change delivered by the Human Resources team. It would typically involve organisational communications, talking points for managers and ensuring that the policy, Frequently Asked Questions and a point of contact are available on the company intranet.
		The words *change* and *transformation* are often used interchangeably. Most times, you can let it pass. But a time may come when you need to call it out, or you are asked about the differences. This short and widely accepted explanation is good to know:

	Chapter	Good to know
		Transformation is when something completely new emerges. It can be explained by the metaphor of a caterpillar emerging as a butterfly over time. The end state (the butterfly) is noticeably different to the initial state (the caterpillar, or even the cocoon).
		Change is a series of incremental alterations or improvements that take place while many other things remain the same. If we apply the metaphor of the caterpillar and butterfly, change results in an improved or different version of the caterpillar.
		It's not surprising that organisational transformation takes longer to achieve, needing a new operating model and organisational design to result in an end state that is completely different.
4	**Through the lens of others**	You can learn a lot from real stories from the trenches to add to what you learn from change management text books. Keep an eye out for LinkedIn posts where new, emerging and experienced change practitioners, such as Dan Paulet, share their experiences. Don't restrict your search to articles. Look out for conversations that have been started in LinkedIn Groups such as Organizational Change Practitioners, Association of Change Management Professionals (ACMP) and Change Management Institute (CMI), where the dialogue is rich in advice, experience and sometimes controversy to spark your curiosity!
		In 2019, Dr Jen Frahm from Conversations of Change, along with Heather Stagl from Enclaria, kicked off the *#changeblogchallenge* - a call to action to all change aficionados to share their wisdom and expertise throughout 2019, in blogs on four nominated themes, one for each quarter. The themes were resistance, communication, change readiness and change leadership. Do a content search on LinkedIn for *#changeblogchallenge* to read the amazing contributions from around the globe.
5	**Roles in change management**	Look beyond the role title; look for the opportunity!

	Chapter	Good to know
6	**Change sponsorship**	Our role as change practitioners is to support the sponsor's vision and commitment to the change by ensuring that our people are ready to adopt the new ways with the right mindset and skillset.
7	**Enterprise change management**	An understanding of change maturity is useful to know. When you join an organisation, you will be able to quickly gauge the level of change maturity. In turn, it will help you navigate conversations and manage expectations. A recruiter may give you an indication as to whether your client or employer has a good level of change maturity in their business... or not!
8	**What they teach you in business school**	Emotional Intelligence (EI) is often referred to as Emotional Quotient (EQ). Many large organisations develop their own change methodology. When this happens, it's common to see a diagram that shows alignment of in-house practice to existing, well-respected change frameworks to validate their approach.
9	**Change capabilities**	Take advantage of free networking events or meetups run by industry bodies in your area. Join social networking conversations inside and outside your organisation. Search 'meetup' on your browser and you will be surprised at how many special interest groups exist and catch up.
10	**Change impact assessments**	The high-level impact assessment can be represented on your visual management board, on a poster size sheet of paper with coloured post-it notes designating high, medium and low. This will generate interest from people passing by, and promote ad hoc conversations that may not have otherwise occurred. For example, a stakeholder or impacted user from Operations may walk past and see that their impact is rated as low, yet they may uncover additional insights that suggest the impact to their business area is high.

	Chapter	Good to know
		You may see change impact levels depicted as *Harvey Balls* - round icons shaded differently to visually represent measures or outcomes. They can be created in PowerPoint or downloaded as icons if you need to use them.
		Before I landed in change management, I had seen my fair share of Harvey Balls but had no idea what they were called. So imagine my confusion when my Change Lead said to me, 'Oh, just use Harvey Balls to show the impact levels.'
11	**Change planning**	As organisations are becoming more agile, change management documentation is becoming lighter and more visual. In more recent times, I've noticed that many change plans start as a *plan on a page* or *change canvas*. Where required, a more detailed change plan builds on this information.
12	**Change communications**	Assign a hashtag to your change initiative for your enterprise social network. Not only does the hashtag make it easy for you and others to search for relevant posts on your project, it also enhances online identity.
		You can download the executive summary of the *Prosci Best Practices in Change Management Benchmarking Report 2018* from the Prosci website.
13	**Stakeholder engagement**	Informal influence is just as effective as formal influence from senior stakeholders.
		Your stakeholder information is confidential data. A stakeholder matrix is a document that often contains sensitive information such as a stakeholder's level of commitment, potential challenges and how they may be addressed by the stakeholder owner. For this reason, make sure this artefact is stored in a place that does not have public access. For example, do *not* store it on your organisation's shared drive. On some projects, this artefact has also been password protected for access by the project team members only.

	Chapter	Good to know
		After running any meetings or workshops on stakeholder commitment, be sure to remove all flipchart sheets, post-it notes, and particularly any notes on a whiteboard - especially check whiteboards that have a rotating writing surface. On more than one occasion, I've found names on whiteboards in meeting rooms that should have been erased.
14	**Learning and performance support**	The impact assessment helps you *begin with the end in mind*. With a view of what is affected in the areas of skills, behaviours, processes and technology required to support the future state, you are able to plan training with that end view in mind.
		Handover to BaU: To ensure there is continued performance support available, the change plan or the learning plan needs to consider the collateral that will be handed over to the impacted business units, and how this knowledge transfer will take place. On the list of the change readiness checklist items, there is often an action to remind the project team and business users to ensure that learning collateral is handed over to the business, so they have documentation on processes and information to train new starters.
15	**Change costs**	Remember, not all change initiatives are the same. Each organisation and change type will carry its own nuances and risks that may require different or additional expenses to those identified here.
16	**Change measures**	**What is hypercare?** Hypercare is the elevated level of support provided just after go-live, typically after a systems implementation. This addresses the increase in support required and promotes confidence in and adoption of the new system. Hypercare may be a dedicated help line, online chat services, and/or the presence of super users to provide on-site assistance.

	Chapter	Good to know
17	**Making change stick**	Once the change has been implemented and the project closed out, as the dedicated change practitioner you're typically rolled off that initiative quite quickly. If you're an external contractor, you're likely to finish up and leave the organisation to pick up your next gig. If you're an internal employee, you will be moved on to the next project to ensure you are fully utilised.
		Who is around to make sure the change is handed over effectively to the change receivers? Who makes sure the change sticks? Make sure you have covered this in your change plan and your handover plan.
18	**Change myths**	A change manager may be a change leader in another role, but it's not a concurrent role.
19	**Change champions**	**The difference between a change champion and a super user:** On larger projects, especially large-scale technology implementations, the roles of *change champion* and *super user* may be separate. On smaller projects, the same person often carries out both roles.
		A *change champion* is often an impacted employee who represents the typical user. The change champion is a change ambassador who acts as the key driver by providing essential input to successfully manage impacted employees through the change curve, via regular two-way communication and support. Change champions support delivery and implementation, as they play a key role in adoption in many capacities, as behaviour models, coaches, trainers, experts, or first points of contact. They are your ears and eyes on the ground. Find them, nurture them and reward them for their contribution to your change initiative.
		A *super user* is focused on the application of a new system or approach, and provides process support for users in the go-live and post go-live period, often called *hypercare*.
20	**Change readiness**	Results from your readiness surveys will uncover useful insights, but the real value and purpose is to drive conversations with your end users and stakeholders.

	Chapter	Good to know
21	**Change resistance**	When impacted users experience threat in response to a change initiative, expect resistance. When there is perceived reward, however, you are more likely to see acceptance.
22	**Change fatigue**	The reasons for the fatigue or 'perceived fatigue' are numerous and are often rooted in experiences with poorly executed change.
23	**Change parables**	Parables are effective ways to introduce sessions and open discussions about change, and to uncover how people are feeling. By exploring response to fictional stories, you can create a safe environment for people to talk, or nudge them to reflect on their reactions and behaviours.
24	**Project management and change management**	A person who carries out the dual roles of project and change manager may be referred to as a *slashie* because of the slash in their title, eg project/change manager. *Slashie* is a term used for someone who carries out more than one role or function.
		A note on interpretation of 'change': Be mindful of the context of the word 'change' AND how it's used in your project.
		On system implementation projects, requests are made and documented for *system changes*.
		In project language, a *change request* is a formal and documented process that details an alteration to what was previously agreed regarding a product or system.
		The term *change request* is often misunderstood as it's described as part of the *change management* process in project literature. However, it is not a change management capability or responsibility. The main thing to note is that a *change request* is neither a people-related change nor the responsibility of the change consultant.
		You may hear reference to the *PMBOK*. This is the abbreviation for the Project Management Body of Knowledge, a resource that details guidelines and terminology for project management. Originally published in 1996, and regularly updated, the PMBOK is widely accepted as the key resource (or bible) for project and program management.

	Chapter	Good to know
25	**Getting on the same page with agile**	Projects using Agile practices alone will not make the organisation agile, as that also requires people to adopt and model the right mindset and behaviours. Agile (yes, big A) project approaches will help, but will not achieve this alone.
26	**Agile change delivery**	If you want to maintain a sequencing approach to change activity, you can continue to use the familiar project activity clusters, such as design, engage, plan, iterate, implement and reflect – but with an adaptive approach, rather than planning and delivering change in the same way for all change initiatives.
		The pressure is on the change practitioner to be increasingly adaptive in their approach. What worked on a project in the bank three years ago is unlikely to hit the mark as an approach on a project in health care today.
27	**Psychological safety**	Whether we are leading others or not, we need to keep in mind that how we act is noticed and has an impact on others - there is a *ripple effect*. This plays a significant role in how safe people feel around others.
28	**Agile change activity**	Agile practices can be applied in all your change planning and your day-to-day engagement with project team members, stakeholders and end users. The practices will promote deeper engagement and co-creation with your stakeholders.
		The more you apply agile practices, the more you will be able to nudge team members to follow, and be more collaborative and transparent.
29	**Change is changing**	In our adaptation to new ways of working, there is a compelling need to demonstrate agility in our mindset, behaviours and practices.
30	**Emerging capabilities**	We need to do things differently to lead and help others manage ongoing change. If you're not already building these emerging capabilities, now is the time to get started because disruptive forces won't wait for you to catch up.

	Chapter	Good to know
31	**Change management meets design thinking**	There is an important benefit for change practitioners when you apply design thinking practices such as running workshops on journey maps: you create a safe place for people to talk about feelings and thoughts. **It legitimises a conversation about emotions that may not occur otherwise.**
32	**Brain-friendly change**	The more we know about how we are hardwired to respond, the more we can do to **make change stick.** It's worth taking the time to find out what provokes a threat response and take steps to reduce it.
33	**Communicate to co-create**	If you are questioned on the value of visual management boards as a powerful communication channel, it may be helpful to remind your stakeholders or project team members that the human brain processes visual information 60,000 times faster than text. You can build a convincing case based on this information.
34	**Staying ahead of the curve**	Self-directed learning is your way to acquire information when you need it, just in time, and to stay ahead of the curve.
35	**What's next?**	The hallmark strength of humanistic values will not lose its relevance. It can be applied to newer approaches, such as agile ways of working, equally as well as it has in the past. Just as organisations and leaders need to be nimble to succeed, change practitioners will need to be equally resilient and adaptive to thrive in our brave new world.

CHAPTER CROSS-CHECK

	Chapter	Related chapters
1	Introduction	All of them!
2	Getting into change management	Change capabilities
3	Types of change	Enterprise change management
		Change champions
		Project management and change management
4	Through the lens of others	Getting into change management
		Change capabilities
		Staying ahead of the curve
5	Roles in change management	Enterprise change management
		Change capabilities
		Project management and change management
6	Change sponsorship	Change planning
7	Enterprise change management	Roles in change management
8	What they teach you in business school	Change planning
		Stakeholder engagement
		Change measures
		Change readiness
		Change resistance
9	Change capabilities	All chapters!
10	Change impact assessments	Change planning
		Learning and performance support

	Chapter	Related chapters
11	Change planning	Change communications
		Stakeholder engagement
		Change impact assessments
		Change costs
		Change measures
		Making change stick
12	Change communications	Stakeholder engagement
		Change measures
		Communicate to co-create
13	Stakeholder engagement	Change planning
		Change communications
		Change readiness
14	Learning and performance support	Change planning
		Change impact assessments
		Change costs
		Change champions
15	Change costs	Change planning
16	Change measures	Change planning
		Making change stick
		Project management and change management
		Communicate to co-create
		Change champions
17	Making change stick	Change planning
		Change measures
		Psychological safety
18	Change myths	Change sponsorship
		Change communications
		Change impact assessments
		Change measures
19	Change champions	Change planning
		Stakeholder engagement
		Learning and performance support
20	Change readiness	Stakeholder engagement
21	Change resistance	Change myths
		Brain-friendly change
		Change management meets design thinking

	Chapter	Related chapters
22	**Change fatigue**	Enterprise change management
		Change resistance
		Agile change activity
		Brain-friendly change
23	**Change parables**	Change communication
24	**Project management and change management**	Change sponsorship
		Change capabilities
		Change planning
25	**Getting on the same page with agile**	Agile change delivery
		Agile change activity
26	**Agile change delivery**	Getting on the same page with agile
		Agile change activity
27	**Psychological safety**	Making change stick
		Agile change delivery
28	**Agile change activity**	Change planning
		Communicate to co-create
29	**Change is changing**	All chapters in part five
30	**Emerging capabilities**	Communicate to co-create
		Change management meets design thinking
		Agile change delivery
		Agile change activity
		Brain friendly change
		Staying ahead of the curve
31	**Change management meets design thinking**	Change measures
		Emerging capabilities
32	**Brain-friendly change**	Change myths
		Change resistance
		Change fatigue
		Emerging capabilities
33	**Communicate to co-create**	Change communications
		Change is changing
		Agile change activity
34	**Staying ahead of the curve**	Roles in change management
		Change capabilities
35	**What's next?**	All of them!

REFERENCES

CHAPTER 2

https://www.prosci.com/

CHAPTER 4

https://www.change-management-institute.com/victoria.

Dan Paulet – LinkedIn:

https://www.linkedin.com/pulse/want-start-career-change-management-daniel-paulet/

https://www.linkedin.com/pulse/career-change-management-ride-so-far-daniel-paulet/

https://www.linkedin.com/in/danielpaulet/

CHAPTER 6

Prosci Best Practices in Change Management 2018 Edition:

https://www.prosci.com/resources/articles/importance-and-role-of-executive-sponsor

https://www.connerpartners.com/roles-and-responsibilities/essential-truths-about-sponsorship

CHAPTER 7

https://www.prosci.com/

Enterprise Change Management: Assessing Change Maturity, blog post on ChangeFirst website:

https://blog.changefirst.com/enterprise-change-management-assessing-change-maturity

CHAPTER 8

Waddell, M., Cummings, T. & Worley, C. (2011), *Organisational change: Development and transformation,* 4th ed., South Melbourne, Cengage Learning.

Kotter, J.P. (1995), Leading Change: Why Transformation Efforts Fail, *Harvard Business Review,* Vol. 73, No. 2, April, pp. 59-67.

Kubler-Ross, E. (1972), On Death and Dying. *JAMA: The Journal of the American Medical Association*, 221(2), pp. 174-179.

https://www.mindtools.com/pages/article/bridges-transition-model.htm

https://www.managementstudyguide.com/scott-and-jaffe-change-model.htm

https://www.tavinstitute.org/projects/field-theory-rule/

https://www.connerpartners.com/frameworks-and-processes/sometimes-people-hate-the-change

Conner, D. & Patterson, R. (1982), Building Commitment to Organisational Change, *Training and development journal,* Vol. 36, No.4, pp. 18-30.

Rogers, E. (1983), *Diffusion of innovations,* 3rd ed., New York, Macmillan.

Kotter, J. P. (2012), *Leading change,* Boston, Harvard Business Review Press.

Kotter, J. P., & Cohen, D. S. (2002), *The Heart of Change: Real-life Stories of How People Change Their Organizations*, Boston, Harvard Business School Press.

https://hbr.org/2012/11/accelerate#

Goleman, D. (1995), *Emotional intelligence: Why It Can Matter More Than IQ*, New York, Bantam Books.

CHAPTER 9

https://www.change-management-institute.com/

CHAPTER 10

Change impact definition by Robert Arnold & Shawn Bohner: https://www.revolvy.com/page/Change-impact-analysis

CHAPTER 11

Kotter, J.P. (1995), Leading Change: Why Transformation Efforts Fail, *Harvard Business Review,* Vol. 73, No. 2, April, pp. 59-67.

Waddell, M., Cummings, T. & Worley, C. (2011), *Organisational Change: Development and Transformation,* 4th ed., South Melbourne, Cengage Learning.

CHAPTER 12

Larkin, T.J. & Larkin, S. (1994), *Communicating Change: Winning Employee Support for New Business Goals,* New York, McGraw Hill.

Prosci Best Practices in Change Management 2018 Edition, p. 150.

https://tim.blog/2009/05/19/vanity-metrics-vs-actionable-metrics/amp/

https://blog.hootsuite.com/social-media-metrics/amp/

CHAPTER 13

Gladwell, M. (2000), *The Tipping Point: How Little Things Can Make a Big Difference,* London, Little Brown & Company.

Conner. D. & Patterson, R. (1982), Building Commitment to Organisational Change, *Training and Development Journal,* Vol. 36, No .4, pp. 18-30.

CHAPTER 15

Change First White Paper (2010), *The ROI of Change Management,* p. 4.

https://www.changefirst.com/resources

CHAPTER 16

Ross, L. (2017), *Hacking for Agile Change: With an agile mindset, behaviours and practices,* Adelaide, Green Hill.

CHAPTER 17

Ross, L. (2017), *Hacking for Agile Change: With an agile mindset, behaviours and practices,* Adelaide, Green Hill.

CHAPTER 18

Frahm, J. Dr. (2017), *Conversations of Change: A Guide to Implementing Workplace Change,* Melbourne, Jennifer Frahm Collaborations.

Mark Hughes (2011), Do 70 Per Cent of All Organizational Change Initiatives Really Fail?, *Journal of change management,* Vol. 11. No. 4, pp. 451-464.

Dr Jen Frahm's article on her Conversations of Change website: https://conversationsofchange.com.au/70-of-change-projects-fail-bollocks1/

Gail Severini article on her website Symphini:

https://symphini.com/time-to-kill-the-phantom-70-failure-rate-quoted-on-transformational-strategy/

Heather Stagl's article on her Enclaria website:

https://www.enclaria.com/2014/06/03/its-time-to-abolish-the-70-change-failure-rate-statistic/

Jason Little's article on his website Lean Change:

https://leanchange.org/2015/05/3-reasons-why-you-should-build-your-own-change-method/

Kotter International – YouTube clip on 'Change management versus change leadership':

https://www.youtube.com/watch?v=SEfgCqnMl5E

CHAPTER 20

Conner. D. & Patterson, R. (1982), Building Commitment to Organisational Change, *Training and Development Journal,* Vol. 36, No. 4, pp. 18-30.

CHAPTER 21

https://www.managementstudyguide.com/scott-and-jaffe-change-model.htm

Covey, S. R. (2004), *The 7 Habits of Highly Effective People: Restoring the Character Ethic*, New York, Free Press.

Rock, D. (2009), Managing with the Brain in Mind, *Strategy & Business,* No. 56, pp. 1-10.

CHAPTER 22

Dr Jen Frahm's article on change fatigue, on her Conversations of Change website:

https://conversationsofchange.com.au/on-change-fatigue/

In this post you will also find the link to the #brainpickers clip where we discuss change fatigue.

CHAPTER 23

Johnson, S. (2002), *Who Moved My Cheese? An Amazing Way to Deal with Change in Your Work and in Your Life,* New York, Putnam.

Kotter, J. P. & Rathgeber, H. (2006), *Our Iceberg is Melting: Changing and Succeeding Under Any Conditions*, New York, St. Martin's Press.

CHAPTER 24

Prosci Best Practices in Change Management 2018 Edition, p. 183.

PMBOK® Guide – Sixth Edition (2017).

CHAPTER 25

Find the Agile Manifesto, values and principles on: www.agilemanifesto.org.

Ross, L. (2017), *Hacking for Agile Change: With an agile mindset, behaviours and practices*, Adelaide, Green Hill.

Frahm, J. Dr. (2017), *Conversations of change: A Guide to Implementing Workplace Change,* Melbourne, Jennifer Frahm Collaborations.

Little, J. (2014), *Lean Change Management: Innovative Practices for Managing Organizational Change,* Happy Melly Express.

CHAPTER 26

The Agile Manifesto, values and principles on www.agilemanifesto.org.

Duckworth, A. (2016), *Grit: The Power of Passion and Perseverance,* New York, Scribner/Simon & Schuster.

FLIMP Studios 5 Guiding Principles for Agile Change Delivery. Search for this animated clip on YouTube by its title.

CHAPTER 27

Kahn, W. A. (1990), Psychological Conditions of Personal Engagement and Disengagement at Work, *Academy of Management Journal,* Vol. 33, No. 4, pp. 692-724.

Edmondson, Amy C. and Lei, Zhike (2014), Psychological Safety: The History, Renaissance, and Future of an Interpersonal Construct, *Annual Review of Organizational Psychology & Organizational Behavior,* Vol. 1, No. 1, pp. 23-43.

https://www.impraise.com/blog/what-is-psychological-safety-and-why-is-it-the-key-to-great-teamwork

https://www.brainpickings.org/2012/01/13/asch-elevator-experiment/

CHAPTER 28

www.benlinders.com Ben is an agile coach who has written a lot about retrospectives. He has presentations on SlideShare too.

CHAPTER 29

Ross, L. (2017), *Hacking for Agile Change: With an agile mindset, behaviours and practices*, Adelaide, Green Hill.

My own white paper found on my website, titled: *So change is the new normal: What change leaders and practitioners need to know in a VUCA world* (2015).

Lawrence, K. (2013), Developing Leaders in a VUCA Environment, *UNC Kenan-Flagler Business School,* White Paper.

Johansen, B. (2009), *Leaders Make the Future: Ten New Leadership Skills for an Uncertain World*, *Academy of Management Executive,* Berrett-Koehler, San Francisco.

https://www.ccl.org/articles/leading-effectively-articles/leadership-skills-for-an-uncertain-world/

Heimans, J. & Timms ,H. (2018), *New Power: How Power Works in Our Hyperconnected World and How to Make It Work for You,* Sydney, Macmillan.

TED Talk by Jeremy Heimans, *What New Power Looks Like*, 2014 on www.ted.com.

CHAPTER 30

My own white paper of emerging capabilities for change mastery found on my website, titled: *High 5 of Change Mastery* (2016).

CHAPTER 31

Brown, T. (2009), *Change by Design*: *How Design Thinking Transforms Organizations and Inspires Innovation,* New York, Harper Collins.

Stanford Institute of Design, d.school, (2012), *Bootcamp Bootleg* - PDF toolkit resource available online on their website www.dschool.stanford.edu.

www.ideo.com

Jump onto my website at lenaross.com.au and look in the resources tab there are media clips. In one clip I talk to Dr Gene Bawden from Monash University on *Where Design Thinking meets Change Management.*

CHAPTER 32

Rock, D. & Schwartz, J. (2006), The Neuroscience of Leadership, *Strategy & Business,* No. 43, pp. 1-10.

Rock, D. (2009), Managing with the Brain in Mind, *Strategy & Business,* No. 56, pp. 1-10.

My own white paper on the neuroscience of change, found on my website in the resources tab, titled: *Navigating through Transformation: A Neuroscience-Based Toolkit for Change,* (2014).

CHAPTER 33

http://leancoffee.org/

Medina, J. (2008), *Brain Rules: 12 Principles for Surviving and Thriving at Work, Home and School,* Seattle, Pear Press.

FLIMP Studios and examples of animated change management clips and interactive PDF documents can be found on their website.

www.flimpstudios.com

Websites for infographic templates:

https://www.canva.com/

https://piktochart.com/

Stepper, J. (2015), *Working Out Loud: For a Better Career and Life*, John Stepper self-published.

CHAPTER 34

Change Management Institute (CMI). http://www.changemanagementreview.com/ - A great site featuring podcasts, events around the globe and articles. Sign up for their weekly newsletter.

Ross, L. (2017), *Hacking for Agile Change: With an agile mindset, behaviours and practices*, Adelaide, Green Hill.

WEB RESOURCES

Dr Jen Frahm

www.conversationsofchange.com.au. This is the online place for change managers looking to build change capability. You will find excellent thought-provoking blogs here. Look for *We need to talk about Agile OCM,* along with Jen's recommended bloggers and tweeps. Her famous podcasts are a must to listen to!

https://drjenfrahm.com/. A place for change leaders where you can also sign up for monthly change leader insights.

Helen Palmer

https://www.questo.com.au/resources/. Helen's created and curated a useful selection of resources for change practitioners who want to mix a design sensibility into how they do things.

https://www.be-selfunlimited.com/. Helen created the unique powerful concept of Self unLimited - a way for individuals to shape and make change in their workscapes. To help the adventurous, there's a book, videos, stories, activities, podcasts and a community of personal change makers.

Andy Cleff

Andy is an experienced and pragmatic agile practitioner who takes teams beyond getting agile, to embracing agile. His chief weapons are often-asked questions, insightful retrospectives and an ability to withstand awkward silences. And if all else fails, beer.

His purpose - what brings him meaning and joy - happens also to be what the world needs most: organisations that are resilient, workforces that experience flow, and teams that solve new complex problems with creative and innovative experiments. His unique passions, curiosity and talent allow him to make a contribution to this need.

Learn more at http://www.andycleff.com/.

Andy is on the Board of Directors of Agile Uprising, a global coalition for agile practitioners. For fabulous podcasts, blogs and to join the discussion visit: http://agileuprising.com/.

COOL TOOLS

Change Design Principles Cards

Helen Palmer from Questo created these cards to stimulate meaningful conversations about change in organisational contexts. The cards don't contain the answers for what to do – rather, they get people thinking about their particular situation to design activities and change strategies that are fit for purpose.

https://www.questo.com.au/change-design-principles/

Self unLimited Value Exchange Cards

Value Exchange is a fresh way of understanding what individuals want from, and contribute to, their workplace. These cards help individuals identify what is personally valuable, and catalyse conversations about taking responsibility for generating that value. A useful tool for change agents and change practitioners helping people to get a positive mindset about organisational changes.

https://www.be-selfunlimited.com/value-exchange/

Chameleon Cards

Check out the Chameleon Cards created by Gilbert Kruidenier and Peter Phan as a tool to help change professionals quickly adapt to their situation and consider their future roles.

https://www.chameleon-cards.com/

FLIMP Studios

Peter Phan from FLIMP Studios cleverly creates customised videos and visuals to help you implement change. On his website you can find sample videos and interactive PDF documents.

https://www.flimpstudios.com/

EXPLORE FREE ONLINE COURSES

There is a list of free online courses at https://www.mooc-list.com/.

Courses from top universities at Coursera - https://www.coursera.org/.

And edx at https://www.edx.org/.

INTERESTS

Facilitation - check out the International Association of Facilitators (IAF) on https://www.iaf-world.org/site/.

INDUSTRY ASSOCIATION WEBSITES

https://www.change-management-institute.com

The lingo used in this book:

Term, Acronym or Abbreviation	What It Means
Agile - little a	Refers to the agile values and principles outlined in the Agile Manifesto, for Agile Software Development.
Agile - capital A	The broader use of the word 'agile', to describe someone who is nimble or quick, ie whose behaviours and mindset are agile, outside the context of Agile Software Development.
Agile Manifesto	Also called the Manifesto for Agile Software Development. Lists four key values and 12 principles to guide an iterative and human-centric approach to software development.
AI	Artificial Intelligence
As is/To be	Terms to describe the current state (as is) and the future state (to be), commonly used when completing change impact assessments.
BaU	Business as Usual
Brown Bag	An informal learning session or meeting that typically takes place at lunchtime.
Business Requirements Document	This document details the business solution for a project, with information on the customer or the user's needs and expectations.

Term, Acronym or Abbreviation	What It Means
C-Suite	Senior executives typically characterised by the word 'chief' in their job title, eg Chief Executive Officer (CEO), Chief Operating Officer (COO), Chief Financial Officer (CFO).
Change Agent	A person who promotes or supports the organisational change.
Change Champion	A change champion is often a representative from an impacted team or business unit who can act as an advocate for the change initiative. Their role is valuable for increasing readiness and adoption.
Change Control	A process to document and manage all changes to a product or system.
Change Initiator	The person in the organisation who has decided to introduce the change.
Change Maturity	A framework to help organisations assess their capability to respond to and introduce change.
Change Receiver	The person who is on the receiving end of the change, often required to adopt new behaviours and/or ways of working.
CIA	Change impact assessment
CIO	Chief Information Officer This role is focused on managing the internal technology infrastructure for the organisation.
CTO	Chief Technology Officer This role is focused on creating technology solutions for external customers.
COP	Community of practice
CX	Customer experience
Delta	The fourth letter in the Greek alphabet, represented as a triangle. Also means variation in mathematics. Often used to represent change.
Design Thinking	An approach that uncovers multiple possibilities before creating a desired solution for customers and/or end users.

Term, Acronym or Abbreviation	What It Means
Downstream System	A software development term to describe a system that *receives* data from another system (the upstream system).
ECMO	Enterprise Change Management Office
ESN	Enterprise social network
EX	Employee experience
FAQs	Frequently Asked Questions
Force Field Analysis	A framework developed by Kurt Lewin that explores factors that drive (support) or restrain (go against) an issue or proposed change.
Gantt Chart	A bar chart that shows the project schedule with tasks and dependencies, line by line.
Gig Economy	A labour market where a large proportion of the workers are short-term contractors, knowledge workers and/or freelancers.
GO/NO GO Decision	A point where a decision is made, based on the readiness checklist, to either go live and proceed with implementation or delay go-live.
Harvey Balls	Round icons used for visual representation of information, such as level of impacts in a change impact assessment.
HCD	Human centred design
Heat Map	A representation of data by colour, where red typically means more intense activity or higher impact, and cooler colours such as green or blue represent lower impact or intensity.
Hypercare	The phase of elevated support provided to impacted users immediately after an implementation to ensure adoption and minimal impacts to productivity and data integrity.
Impact Category	The type of impact an organisation or business unit will experience in the typical categories of people, technology, process and customer. Some organisations may have additional categories unique to their own business environment.
Impact Level	The anticipated intensity of the impact on a business unit or team, categorised as none, low, medium or high.
IoT	Internet of Things

Term, Acronym or Abbreviation	What It Means
Journey Map	A design thinking tool that uncovers the customer's interaction with the product or service at various touch-points, highlighting potential pain points and opportunities for improvement.
Kanban	A visual representation (such as a board) of work in progress: what work has started, been completed and is yet to commence.
LNA/TNA	Learning Needs Analysis/Training Needs Analysis
Lean Coffee	A structured meeting where the agenda is decided by the participants.
Lunch and Learn	An informal learning session that typically takes place at lunchtime.
Machine Learning (ML)	Where a machine applies Artificial Intelligence (AI) to continually learn and improve its own performance and responses, without the need for ongoing programming.
Microlearning	Bite-sized learning that takes place in small activities, such as watching a 5-10 minute clip.
MVP	Minimum viable product. A deliverable (product or service) that contains sufficient features to deliver value and/or objectives, often to seek user feedback for further refinement.
Neuroscience	The study of brain activity and its impact on behaviour.
New Power	A term coined by Jeremy Heimans and Henry Timms to describe how power has changed in a hyper-connected world from traditional hierarchical models to more collab-orative, shared ones. Heimans and Timms have written a book by the same name.
OCM	Organisational change management
Persona	A composite character that represents characteristics of a customer segment or user group, such as demographic and psychographic characteristics.
PCI	People Centred Implementation - Change First's registered change methodology.
PIR	Post-implementation review

Term, Acronym or Abbreviation	What It Means
PMBOK	Project Management Body of Knowledge
PLN	Personal learning network
Prosci	A contraction of the words 'professional' and 'science'. Prosci is a US-based company that carries out extensive research in change management.
QRG	Quick reference guide
RACI	Responsible, Accountable, Consult, Inform
RAG	Red, Amber, Green
RAM	Responsibility assignment matrix
Retrospective	An agile retrospective is a review meeting held at the end of each iteration or deliverable, for the team to reflect on what went well, what went less well, and to document improvement actions for next time.
Risk Register	A tool that documents project risks and the actions taken to address those risks.
Robotics	The field and industry relating to the design and development of robots.
SCARF	Status, Certainty, Autonomy, Relatedness, Fairness. A framework developed by neuroscientist David Rock to describe how people interact and respond to threat and reward triggers.
SDLC	Software Development Life Cycle. A software engineering approach to design, develop and test software.
Slack	Enterprise social network for colleagues to share information and collaborate.
Slashie	A person performing more than one role, such as the project manager who is also carrying out the role of change manager to be project/change manager.
SME	Subject matter expert
Sponsor	The project sponsor is the person in the organisation with the overall accountability to ensure that the project's business benefits are delivered.

Term, Acronym or Abbreviation	What It Means
STEM	Science, Technology, Engineering, Mathematics. A set of four subjects that together are valued as a thinking approach for problem solving in a digital world.
Super User	In a change management context, a super user is someone who has been upskilled in the new processes and/or technology ahead of the change implementation so they can support new users for go-live. Their role is valuable for increasing readiness and adoption.
SWOT	Strengths, Weaknesses, Opportunities and Threats
TOM	Target operating model
Triple Constraint	Represents the three constraints of time, cost and scope. Ssometimes referred to as the project management triangle.
Upstream system	In technology, the upstream system is the one that *sends* data to a downstream system.
User Scenario	A description of one way an end user (customer or employee) might interact with an existing and/or future service or product, such as an application or a website.
UX	User experience
Vanity Metrics	A term typically used for social media measures that focus on the number of followers. These metrics appear impressive but are less relevant to actual engagement levels and business performance.
VUCA	Volatility, Uncertainty, Certainty, Ambiguity
Wagile	A word that has been made up to describe a combination of Waterfall and Agile practices applied to a project.
Waterfall	A linear and sequenced project approach where the commencement of each distinct phase is dependent on the previous one.
WIIFM	Acronym for "what's in it for me?"
WOL	Working out loud
Yammer	Enterprise social network for colleagues to share information and collaborate. Yammer is a platform owned by Microsoft.

ACKNOWLEDGEMENTS

It's a curious thing, writing a book. You learn a great deal about yourself, and your stamina, resilience, grit and patience. Even more importantly, you learn a LOT about the people around you who champion and support you. Your cheer squad, your tribe and your family become more apparent and present. They show their true colours.

I was lucky to find a cheer squad and tribe members who go beyond any expectation. They generously shared stories so the book can represent a range of experiences, not just my own.

To my reviewers - they say when you want something done, ask a busy person, and that I did! Time is a precious resource and when someone takes time to read a book in its early iteration, they have given you a very generous gift. Not just of their time, but their thoughts and most valuable feedback. My reviewers are some of the busiest people in my peer community and this book has been shaped by this gift of time from them. They are Gilbert Kruidenier, Joanne Rinaldi, Sharon King, Anna Kiss-Gyorgy and Dr Jen Frahm.

A second and special thanks to Dr Jen Frahm, who has not only reviewed the entire manuscript but also wrote the Foreword. And so much more... from crossing paths when we both worked at NAB, to #brainpickers, to a joint book launch in 2017, and most recently the Agile Change Leadership

Institute. It's been a great ride! With each brainstorm Jen continues to share her insight and pragmatism to inspire and push me beyond comfort zones to keep on creating.

To the readers of my first book *Hacking for Agile Change* - thank you for urging me to do it again.

To Dan Paulet - for permission to reproduce his fabulous LinkedIn posts that document his candid experiences in change management.

To my close family members who know me so well - they were the ones who knew when to interrupt me because they clearly saw what I could not - the need for fresh air or coffee... or both!

To my offspring - I've realised that I've raised Anthony and Justine to be bold with feedback and candour. They are the ones who bravely tell me when my writing (and housekeeping) has gone off the rails.

To the greatest 'nudger' of all, my other half, Grant - he pokes, he teases, he challenges, he reviews drafts without complaint, and somehow manages to maintain a beginner's mindset.

ABOUT THE AUTHOR

Lena Ross is an experienced and mildly disruptive change consultant with a reputation for valuable content creation and speaking at conferences and events. Since establishing her consulting practice in 2016, #changehacks, Lena has been invited to share her expertise as a guest blogger, panellist, commentator and podcaster on the future of change management and emerging capabilities.

Lena's work draws on the latest thinking in change management from areas such as agile approaches, design thinking, the future of work, digital and hardwired human behaviour. Her future-forward views and approaches to collaborative learning, disruptive communication channels, and human-centred applications to delivering change are all designed for deep engagement and co-creation. With Dr Jen Frahm from Conversations of Change, Lena set up the #brainpickers youtube channel, where they talk about hot topics in change management, with tips for leaders and change practitioners.

Her experience is well complemented by her relevant tertiary qualifications, such as a Master of Business Administration (MBA) from Monash University. Within this context, she is able to apply sound academic discipline to the development of practical solutions.

Lena's services include onsite consulting, workshop facilitation, coaching and speaking. Together, Jen and Lena co-founded of the **Agile Change Leadership Institute** and have developed unique agile learning programs such as *Change Pick n Mix* and the *Certificate of Agile Change Leadership,* based on the principles of bite-sized brain-friendly learning. They have consulted to and coached clients across numerous industries and geographies, with a recent engagement in Silicon Valley.

Born and bred in Melbourne, Australia, Lena is often spotted balancing the city life with the serene energy of Daylesford, in the beautiful spa region of Victoria, Australia.

Her first book, *Hacking for Agile Change,* was published in July 2017.

To find out more about Lena's work and her resources, visit her website on www.lenaross.com.au.

Curious? Check out these products...

The perfect way to complement this book is
with the **#changeessentials**
online learning program with **LENA ROSS**

ANYTIME... ANYWHERE

It doesn't matter where you're located, or when you want to learn.

This online learning program with short learning clips means you can learn when and where it works for you. You'll get:

- 12 months access to learning content
- Online clips you can watch as often as you like during the access period
- Downloadable templates, tools and infographics designed for the modern change practitioner.

Enterprise packages also available for change teams.

Head over to my website for more details:

www.lenaross.com.au.

Hacking for Agile Change:
With an agile mindset,
behaviours & practices
by Lena Ross

A must-have guide for every change leader and practitioner, with over 50 practical and proven change hacks you can apply in your change initiative on any project type and in any organisation.

This book will help you:

- Define agile as a business capability
- Try new change management approaches, with examples and practical tips on how to get cut-through
- Uncover more ways to lead and manage human-centric change
- Consider new ways of working and other emerging trends in your change delivery
- Broaden your capability and future-proof your career.

Head over to my website and click on the shopping icon to go to the online store.

www.lenaross.com.au

or you can find it on Amazon. Also available in eBook.

A deck of 52 cards that you can use as a tactile tool to nudge your mindset

mindfulness hacks for busy people

These days, we seem to be busier than ever before. We're often too busy to pause and think about what we've accomplished, how we perceive the world around us, and what we have the potential to achieve.

The cards are more than just conversation starters - they are mindfulness hacks.

When you **ponderfy**, you: reflect | connect | provoke | plan | visualise

Anyone can **ponderfy**... anytime... anywhere...

facilitators | team leaders | coaches | counsellors | friends | individuals

Head over to my website and click on the shopping icon to go to the online store.

www.lenaross.com.au

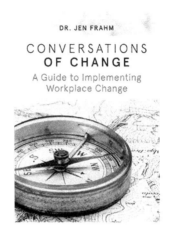

Conversations of Change: A Guide to Implementing Workplace Change
by Dr Jen Frahm

Managing change in a workplace can be a difficult process. Your focus should be on the opportunity it presents, not the problem that's been created. *Conversations of Change* is a practical guide that navigates experienced and inexperienced managers alike through the process of identifying, creating and measuring real and effective change.

We know that the field of change management is complex, often obtuse, jargon-laden, and difficult to navigate at speed without a guide.

Managers are increasingly expected to initiate, lead and execute change in the workplace. Often with little knowledge or experience of change management.

Conversations of Change: A Guide to Implementing Workplace Change will make it easy for managers to work out what they need to do, who they need to help them, and what to consider in their workplace change efforts. In doing so it offers the opportunity to build their change capability and their team's change capability. It's also a gold mine for those who want to fast track a career in organisational change.

www.conversationsofchange.com.au/products/

The change leadership book bundle

Can't decide which book you should read? We've made it easy for you.

Equip yourself with *Hacking for Agile Change* by Lena Ross and *Conversations of Change* by Dr Jen Frahm in one convenient bundle.

Both books are invaluable resources for anyone involved in the change process. For change practitioners who are just starting out and need to find a way through, to veteran change practitioners who want to stay on target, *Hacking for Agile Change* and *Conversations of Change* are must-have resources for any change leader's library.

NOTE: Price includes postage and handling costs to Australia only. Overseas buyers - please contact us for alternative arrangements.

Head over to my website and click on the shopping icon to go to the online store.

www.lenaross.com.au

Agile Change Leadership Institute

New ways of working mean new ways of learning and leading

brings you:

CERTIFICATE OF AGILE CHANGE LEADERSHIP

Learn what you need to know about leading change in agile environments –
when you want it, where you want it, and at a pace that suits you.

The unique learning approach means that you learn in bite-sized pieces,
practise in real time and reflect and share. The six modules, each with three
clips, are on topics that are particularly relevant to change leaders. Content
is delivered online, with experiments to apply in your workplace, along with
reflective learning exercises to build an iterative learning mindset.

This program will make you more confident in your ability to be a sponsor or a
leader of transformation.

CHANGE PICK N MIX

An agile learning program you design from various elements to build change capability in bite-sized chunks. The foundation workshop covers leading change in challenging conditions; you then pick n mix the additional elements such as coaching clinics, further workshop and focus talks, online learning bumps, and change nudges (micro content to nudge thinking about change and agility).

AGILE CHANGE ADVENTURER WORKSHOP

You've got a change management team that needs to get up to speed with working on agile projects. Your existing change processes and frameworks feel too heavy and slow! You're at risk of irrelevance. Agile change management can be really liberating - but you do need to take time to work out how you can adapt your current practice and what else you need to learn.

Let us run an in-house Agile Change Adventurer day for you!

More information:

Website: **https://agilechangeinstitute.com.au/**
Facebook: **https://www.facebook.com/agilechangeleadershipinstitute/**
LinkedIn: **And follow our page on LinkedIn - Agile Change Leadership Institute.**

#changeessentials

It's a small world!

You can find me and connect on:

Website   lenaross.com.au

Facebook   https://business.facebook.com/changehacks/

LinkedIn   www.linkedin.com/in/lenaross/

Twitter   @lenaemelyross

Instagram   @changeessentials

Newsletter   Head over to the CONTACT page on my website to subscribe
                 to my newsletter.

Lightning Source UK Ltd.
Milton Keynes UK
UKHW020744280722
406510UK00010B/742